STALIN
AND THE
SOVIET UNION

Jim Grant
Series editor: Christopher Culpin

 LONGMAN

CONTENTS

PART ONE

INTRODUCTION

Josef Stalin is one of the key figures of twentieth-century world history. Like Mao, Hitler and Mussolini, he came from humble origins yet managed to acquire unprecedented power. He presided over cataclysmic changes in Russia, the repercussions of which touched most of the world through the Russian victory in the Second World War, the Cold War and the spread of communist ideas. Currently, Stalin's historic stock is low. Often bracketed with Hitler, Pol Pot and Mussolini, he has been demonised because of the millions who died under his regime and the stifling influence of 'Stalinism' on Soviet life. Many writers have labelled his rule, 'totalitarian'. At the same time, Stalin's ruthlessness is often credited with enabling the Union of Soviet Socialist Republics (USSR) to defeat Nazi Germany and with dragging Russia from the age of wooden ploughs into the space race. Apparently condemned to the 'dustbin of history' by Mikhail Gorbachev's reforms and the subsequent collapse of the USSR in 1990, Stalin's picture has recently been paraded through Moscow by those who miss the order, purpose and status he brought to Russia. As Russians react against the ethnic disintegration of their empire, rising crime and 'bullying' by America, we may yet see a revival of Stalin's historical fortunes.

There is little doubt that Stalin was a contradictory figure and difficult to interpret. His secrecy ensured that few explicit records of his thoughts survive. He outlasted the other leading dictators of the 1930s and seemed to concentrate real power more effectively than any of them; apparently disposing of potential rivals or successors ruthlessly. At the same time, the USSR gained a reputation for inefficiency, conspiracies and economic failure. What criteria should we use to judge Stalin?

As you look through the outline of events in this chapter start to think about the following questions.

◢ How did Stalin become supreme in Russia?

◢ How valid is it to call the USSR a 'totalitarian state'?

◢ Why did so many Soviet citizens support Stalin?

◢ How far did 'Stalinism' differ from Lenin's Communism?

◢ What shaped Soviet policy: personality, economics or ideology?

◢ How can we evaluate Stalin's impact on the Russian people?

◢ Why do some Russians remember him with nostalgia?

Political events		Economics
End of Civil War. Soviet occupation of Georgia	1921	Famine. New Economic Policy
USSR set up. Stalin becomes Party General Secretary	1922	
	1923	
Death of Lenin. Defeat of Trotsky	1924	Success of NEP
Defeat of Kamenev and Zinoviev. Stalin and Bukharin rule USSR	1925	Concessions to peasants
Defeat of 'United Opposition'.	1926	
War scare. Expulsion of 'Leftists'	1927	Shortages in grain supply
First 'show trials'	1928	Start of grain requisition. First 5-Year Plan
Defeat of Bukharin and 'Rightists'. Stalin becomes sole ruler	1929	Forced collectivisation. War against the *kulaks*
Show trials	1930	
	1931	Strict labour discipline introduced
Suicide of Stalin's wife, Alliluyeva	1932	Famine
Party purge	1933	Second 5-Year Plan
Assassination of Kirov	1934	
	1935	Stakhanovite Movement
New Constitution. Trial and execution of Old Bolshevik leaders	1936	
Height of the Purges, including execution of Army leaders	1937	
Trial and execution of Bukharin.	1938	Third 5-Year Plan focuses on defence

Figure 1 Even after the collapse of Communism, some Russians continue to commemorate Stalin's achievements.

Non-Aggression Pact with Germany. Occupation of Poland	**1939**	
Assassination of Trotsky.	**1940**	
German invasion	**1941**	Shifting of industry east
German victories	**1942**	
Soviet victories at Stalingrad and Kursk	**1943**	
Soviet invasion of Eastern Europe	**1944**	
Red Army captures Berlin	**1945**	
Wartime allies fall out	**1946**	Rebuilding the economy begins.
Start of 'Cold War'	**1947**	
	1948	
Atomic bomb developed	**1949**	
Korean War	**1950**	
	1951	Fifth 5-Year Plan
	1952	
Death of Stalin	**1953**	

Russia in 1924

Communist government

By the time of Lenin's death in 1924, the **Communists** had eliminated political opposition in Russia. After defeating the various 'White' armies in the Civil War, most of the former territories of the Tsarist Empire had been 'persuaded' to join the Soviet Union (USSR). The Red Army had suppressed nationalist movements in Georgia and Central Asia. The only difference between the Tsarist Empire and the USSR was the loss of territory in the west to Poland, Finland and the Baltic States.

KEY TERM

Communists were originally called Bolsheviks. The Bolshevik Party changed its name to the Communist Party in 1918. Vladimir Lenin and the Bolsheviks were followers of the C19th German philosopher, Karl Marx. He taught that history was made up of a series of struggles between classes. Since the dawn of civilisation, one 'ruling class' after another had controlled the sources of wealth or 'means of production' and used this power to dominate other classes. Marx saw the Industrial Revolution of the C18th and C19th as a time when capitalists (bankers, factory owners *etc.*), who were drawn from the bourgeoisie (middle class), took power from the old aristocracy, whose wealth had been in land. The bourgeoisie became wealthy by exploiting their workers: the 'proletariat'. Eventually the proletariat would organise themselves to overthrow capitalism and become the new ruling class. Their society, where no one would be exploited, was called Communism. Marx expected this revolution to occur in the most industrialised nations. Lenin broke with other 'Marxists' in arguing that it was possible to move straight to Communism, without waiting for the 'bourgeois revolution'.

The Soviet people

Most of the 160 million people of the USSR lived west of the Ural mountains, particularly concentrated in the Moscow–Leningrad area and the rich soils of the Ukraine (see Figure 2). Barely half of Soviet citizens were Russians; the rest belonged to over 90 different ethnic groups. The West contained large minorities of Ukrainians, Georgians and Europe's largest Jewish population. In Central Asia, Moslems, including Uzbeks and Kazakhs, predominated. Siberia and the North was thinly populated. Although officially atheist, many in rural areas remained religious. The USSR was officially Russian speaking, but barely half were native speakers. Even less could read Russian. Illiteracy rates exceeded 50% for men and 80% for women. Many political leaders came from minority groups (particularly Jews) since they had been discriminated against and persecuted under the Tsars. This had involved attempts to 'Russify' non-Russians by suppressing their language and culture. Lenin had promised them equal rights in the USSR.

Peasants

80% of the population were peasant farmers. Many retained land held in Tsarist times or seized from landlords during the Revolution. Peasants varied enormously in their individual wealth, with several million owning no land at all, but they differed even more from modern farmers. They were very traditional in outlook, religious and rarely interested in events beyond their village. They were deeply suspicious of, and resistant to, governments which had always taxed them, taken their grain and conscripted their sons. Isolated by poor communications and largely illiterate, it is unlikely that many were aware of the political battles taking place in Moscow and Petrograd. However, ambitious peasants who had taken advantage of Tsarist land reforms to develop independent farms, were angered by Bolshevik decrees of 1917 which restored the power to village communes.

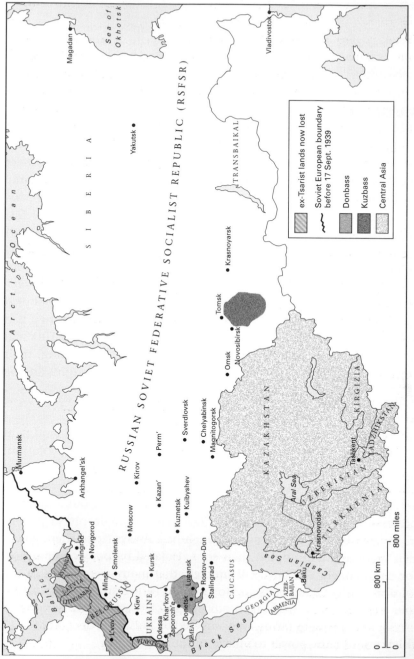

Figure 2 The Soviet Union in the 1930s

Very few had obeyed Bolshevik calls to pool their land to form *collective farms* or cooperatives, preferring to own land as individual or household groups. These 25 million farms, or holdings, were mostly poor and backward, many villages operating a three-field rotation system of planting with one field always fallow. Individual peasant holdings would be made up of strips within these fields. Horses and humans provided power. 74% of grain was sown by hand and nearly half harvested with sickle or scythe. There were twice as many wooden ploughs as metal ones. Machines and chemical fertilisers were almost unheard of. Horses and ox carts provided transport. Peasants were largely self-sufficient, only around 25 per cent produced a surplus to sell at market.

KEY TERM

Collective farms were the Communist model for agricultural production. They came in two basic forms:
- On State-owned land, the *Sovkhoz* would produce crops needed by the state (*e.g.* cotton) and employ workers who would be paid wages.
- Individual peasants voluntarily pooled their land and farming equipment to form *Kolkhoz*. These sold produce to the Government and shared the profits.

A 'peasant society'

Date	Approx. population	Urban	Rural
1915	159 million	28	131
1926	165 million	33	132
1940	194 million	63	131
1950	178 million	69	109
1955	194 million	86	108

Workers

The proletariat were the class which the Bolsheviks claimed to represent. They formed around 10 per cent of the population and were concentrated in a few urban areas – such as Moscow, Petrograd and Kiev – and in mining regions such as the Donbas and around Perm' in the Urals (see Figure 2). They included factory workers, miners, railway workers and a large number employed in workshops. They often lived in very poor housing with many health and social problems. Although

Russian industry lagged behind the West, some large, modern enterprises had been established in metal processing and arms manufacture. The concentrated populations of workers enabled radical ideas to spread during the last Tsarist years. Working-class anger at poor conditions, low wages and food shortages fuelled the revolutions of 1905 and 1917.

A middle class?
Unlike Western Europe, Russia had not developed a large middle class. There were small numbers of professionals and a wealth of Tsarist bureaucrats (the hated 'chinovniks'). Although many of Russia's capitalists had been foreigners, there were also some factory managers and engineers. These people had never had much political influence until the Provisional Government of 1917. Since then their numbers had been reduced by civil war and exile. This was also true of the old aristocratic ruling class of landlords and higher officials. In 1924 the most educated (the **intelligentsia**) were the remaining children of these groups. These included some of the Bolshevik leaders, e.g. Lenin and Kollontai.

In the early 1920s new groups emerged, including small traders (**Nepmen**) and the Party Officials (*Apparatchiks*), appointed to administer the country and the economy. There was also the military, the higher ranks achieved by some sons of workers during the Civil War. Unfortunately, there were insufficient educated Communist workers to fill these posts so Lenin continued to employ managers, engineers and scientists from the old anti-Bolshevik intelligentsia, although he appointed Political Commissars to watch over them. Until the 1930s these people dominated the universities, planning commissions and industry. Communist workers had to take instructions from them.

Government
The USSR was a federation of states (*e.g.* Ukraine, Georgia). Each had its own government and theoretically could leave if it wanted. In fact, these governments were also taken over by Communists who followed the Russian party line. After the collapse of the left-wing Coalition Government in 1918, Russia became a one-party state with only the Communist Party permitted. However, because Lenin had been forced

to employ non-Party members in administrative posts, many officials had previously been the Bolsheviks' 'enemies'! The population made their views known via the Soviets (workers' councils) at local, regional and national level. Communists held a majority on the Soviets so representation was more theoretical than real. Government Ministers, or **Commissars**, were all drawn from the Bolshevik leaders who had seized power in 1917. The most important of these leaders met in a council called *Sovnarkom*. One key problem faced by Soviet governments was their lack of influence in rural areas and the lack of commitment among office-holders (see Figure 3).

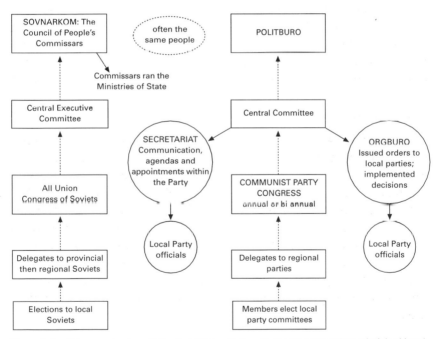

Figure 3 Parallel power structures in the Soviet Union. Both systems were democratic in principle although not in practice. Party members monopolised the upper levels of Soviet government.

The Party

Communist Party Membership was open to all proletarians and rose from 26,000 in early 1917 to about 500,000 by the early 1920s. Many older members were used to debating policy with the leadership and had disagreed with Lenin over the way the country and economy was run during the Civil War. These members, mainly on the left of the Party, wanted greater democracy and real workers' control. In 1921 Lenin lost patience and expelled them for 'factionalism'. Many expelled were peasants which reinforced the urban bias in the Party. However, some dissidents remained, e.g. Preobrazenski who called for rapid industrialisation.

In the USSR, to ensure loyalty, those appointed to official posts or promoted were largely Party members. Similarly, those elected in the soviets and regions were Communists. This meant that being a party member offered promotion. As a result, recruits joined for selfish, as much as ideological, reasons. It also meant that the Party Secretaries had much influence, since they could appoint people to jobs and support particular candidates. The Party General Secretary was Josef Stalin and his two deputies were Vyacheslav Molotov and Valerian Kuibyshev. The official newspaper, *Pravda* ('Truth'), also belonged to the Party. Nikolai Bukharin was its editor. The top council of the Party was the **Politburo**. Lenin never clarified the relationship between Party and State. Although he ran the USSR from *Sovnarkom* by the mid-1920s the Politburo had become the seat of power. Part of the problem was that Marxists expected the State to 'wither away' once Communism was established. Similarly, Lenin had established the Bolshevik (later Communist) Party to organise the Revolution on behalf of the proletariat. However, once power had been secured, it was clear that both still had a role to play. Under Stalin, the Party and its Congress would become vital as the source of his support and legitimacy.

Policy
To provide high living standards for all, the Communists needed an industrial society with workers, not capitalists, taking the profits. When the Bolsheviks seized power in October 1917, their aim was for world revolution, after which richer workers' states would help more backward societies, including Russia, to industrialise. That hadn't happened. There was no blueprint for achieving Communism in a poor and hungry country, surrounded by hostile neighbours. This meant plenty of scope for debate.

In response to the destruction of the economy in the Civil War, lack of foreign help and the risk of new revolts, Lenin made a tactical retreat from Marxist ideas. His **'New Economic Policy'** (NEP) put large-scale industrialisation and social changes on hold, while making concessions to peasants and small businesses in order to feed and clothe the country. Lenin died without leaving a clear plan for the next step (Figure 4). His successors fell out trying to find one.

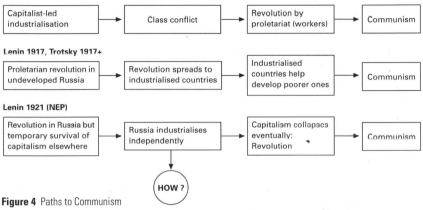

Figure 4 Paths to Communism

Chronological survey of Stalin's Russia

1 The power struggle, 1924–9

After Lenin died in January 1924, the task of developing a new strategy fell to a new collective leadership. Its most important members were Trotsky (the most prominent), Zinoviev, Kamenev, Stalin and Bukharin (Lenin's favourite). Lenin left a testament which evaluated each of these men and pointed out their strengths and weaknesses. For Stalin, it was particularly damning; an attached clause called for his removal.

Before Lenin's death, his successors had already fallen out, some jealous of Trotsky's position and fame. They resented him and feared that he might seize power as a military dictator. Ignoring Lenin's wishes, Kamenev and Zinoviev protected Stalin, forming a 'triumvirate' to attack Trotsky. Trotsky publicised his own ideas in 1924, calling for 'permanent revolution' (spreading revolution abroad) and rapid industrialisation. This apparent break with Lenin's policy was poorly timed. Stalin countered with a defence of 'Leninism', while he and Bukharin put forward the idea of 'Socialism in one country' (peace and concentrating on Russia). Meanwhile, Bukharin sought to demonstrate that the NEP (which many saw as a retreat from Communism) was, in fact, a Marxist economic strategy. By 1925 Trotsky was sidelined.

The next four years saw manoeuvring within the leadership. Stalin, allied to Bukharin, won but in 1929 turned on his ally and became the unchallenged leader. The losers were expelled from the Party.

2 The revolution from above, 1929–41

Stalin launched a period of massive and rapid change which is the main concern of this book. Three linked themes make up this process: ◢ industrialisation, ◢ collectivisation, ◢ repression.

Industrialisation

The **Five Year Plans** set huge targets for industry and agriculture. The first Five Year Plan (1928–33) developed infrastructure and built new cities and industries in Central Russia. The second Five Year Plan (1933–8) was more realistic and saw the development of engineering, power and metal industries. The third Five Year Plan was dominated by rearmament to face the Nazi Germany threat. The plans did not meet their targets, but the Soviet Union became an industrial superpower. However, while growth was impressive, life for the population was grim. Living standards fell and millions died in the famine and terror of the 1930s.

Collectivisation

Finance for industrialisation came from squeezing the peasants. In 1928 grain was requisitioned to feed the workers. Those resisting were dubbed '**kulaks**' and in 1929 Stalin launched a war to eliminate them. Peasants were rapidly forced into collective farms where grain could be centrally controlled to supply towns or to provide exports to pay for technology. Peasants resisted by burning their possessions and slaughtering their livestock. The outcome of this process by 1932 was famine. Collectivisation was a disaster for agriculture and Stalin had to make concessions to the peasants to prevent complete collapse.

Repression

Among workers there was considerable enthusiasm. Volunteers helped construct new industrial towns from scratch in an attempt to create a new society. However, fear was also used when things went wrong. Managers who failed to meet targets were labelled 'wreckers'. Foreigners helping on industrial projects were accused of spying or sabotage. Public show trials were held of those accused. Harsh labour laws were used to discipline workers. Criticism was silenced as a 'cultural revolution' attempted to eliminate alternative ways of thinking. Millions were arrested, sent to prison camps (*gulags*) or shot. The Communist Party itself was devoured in the 'Purges' (see box).

The Purges

In 1934 Stalin claimed victory for his revolution but there was a political cost. Increasingly, dissent was interpreted as disloyalty. Everyone had to observe the official 'Stalinist' line. Opponents were labelled 'enemies of the people'. At best they were sacked, at worst they joined the 'Kulaks' in the gulags, or were executed. The old Bolshevik leaders were tried and the Party was purged of anyone suspected of deviance. Only loyal Stalinists were to remain and many of them were to fall victim after 1934. In that year, Sergei Kirov, a popular leader from Leningrad, was assassinated. Mass arrests followed and over the next four years the Secret Police rounded up hundreds of thousands more. In 1937, most of the Red Army leadership were executed for treason. This triggered an orgy of killing in which thousands of innocent people were shot. By the time Bukharin was tried and executed in 1938, only Stalin and Trotsky survived from the Bolshevik leaders of 1917. Trotsky was assassinated by Stalin's agents in Mexico in 1940.

---

3 The Great Patriotic War, 1941–5

Hitler invaded Russia in June 1941. Stalin was taken by surprise and his armies defeated. The Germans narrowly failed to take Moscow and began a two-year siege of Leningrad. In 1942 the victorious Germans swept across southern Russia executing 'racial enemies' in the territories they conquered. The winter of 1942–3 brought the turning-point. Stalin refused to allow the city of Stalingrad to fall and eventually the

German Army there surrendered. The cold winter halted the Germans while the Russians began to swamp them with new armies. After the Soviet victory in the Battle of Kursk in 1943, the Germans were rolled back through eastern Europe and in May 1945 the Red Army took Berlin. The Soviet Union had defeated Nazi Germany and Stalin, as leader, became its hero. The cost had been terrible. Estimates of Russian dead are 20 million, while much of the country had been devastated.

4 The final years, 1946–53

Postwar Five Year Plans focused on reconstruction and arms. The USSR had a new rival in the USA, and the two **'superpowers'** vied for influence after 1945 in an escalating **'Cold War'**. The Red Army was larger, but the Americans had the atomic bomb. Stalin exploded his first atomic bomb in 1949, starting an arms race which ended in the late 1980s.

The cult of Stalin increased. He had saved Russia. His position was unchallenged, but this did not bring internal peace. Whole ethnic groups who had helped the Germans were exiled, returning prisoners-of-war were sent to Siberia because they might be contaminated with western ideas and the Purges returned. These were not quite up to the levels of the 1930s, but hundreds of thousands more were locked up in the *gulags*. Leading Communists were also not immune.

5 Aftermath

As in 1924 there was no clear succession and a collective leadership took over. Finally in 1956, Nikita Khrushchev emerged as leader, condemning Stalin for some of the terrible things which had happened under him. However, Khrushchev's **De-Stalinisation** policies were unpopular in some quarters and he too was removed.

In 1964 Leonid Brezhnev partly resurrected the cult of Stalin. Not until the Gorbachev 1980s did the Party finally reject Stalin, moving back towards the ideas of NEP and Bukharin. However, Gorbachev too ran out of time and the Soviet Union which Stalin had built collapsed. The Communist Party lost power to Boris Yeltsin and the capitalist governments of the early 1990s. All over the world (except China), commentators condemned Stalin and his system. Communism was declared to be dead. However, in January 1996 a reformed Communist Party topped the poll in the Russian elections.

Josef STALIN *1880–1953*

Born into a poor Georgian family in the Caucasus region of the Tsar's Empire, **Joseph Djugashvili** had a hard upbringing. Beaten by his drunken father, he was sent by his mother to train to be a priest. At the seminary he learned Russian and Russian history. He rebelled against the strict discipline and was expelled. He drifted into revolutionary Marxist groups, finally joining the Bolsheviks. An activist, he was often arrested for agitation or robbery. He demonstrated his determination by escaping from Siberia three times. Some say he also worked for the secret police at times. Stalin is virtually the only widely-known figure from Russia in the 1930s. However, he shared power with Bukharin for five years and worked with two generations of new leaders during his 29 years at the top. These 'Stalinists' were not mere puppets and had a considerable influence on events.

Nikolai BUKHARIN *1888–1938*

A teacher's son and a Bolshevik activist from his teens, he was a leading thinker and writer who played a leading role in Moscow during the Revolution. Lenin nominated Bukharin to share power with Dzerzhinski if he and Trotsky were killed in the fighting. Initially on the left of the Party, Bukharin disagreed with Lenin over many issues although he was close to him by his death. In the Politburo from 1924, he moved 'right' to became the chief defender of NEP and ruled the USSR with Stalin until 1928. His writings provide the alternative direction Communism could have taken instead of Stalinism. Defeated by Stalin, he was allowed back into the Party in the mid-1930s and drafted the 1936 Constitution. He was executed on false charges in 1938.

'MOLOTOV', Vyacheslav Scriabin *1890–1986*

He was a long-time Bolshevik activist who worked closely with Stalin once he reached high office. As Deputy Secretary, he helped Stalin in his rise during the 1920s by taking over Leningrad for him and he became Premier in 1930. As Commissar for Foreign Affairs he concluded the 1939 Pact with Hitler and was the top Soviet negotiator during the Second World War and early Cold War. Stalin's close friend until the late 1940s, his harsh methods and loyalty earned him the nickname 'Stalin's bludgeon'. Despite his Jewish wife being imprisoned, he outlived Stalin and remained in the Politburo until 1957.

Grigori ORDZHONIKIDZE *1886–1937*

A fellow Georgian, Ordzhonikidze was linked to Stalin from his early days as a Bolshevik. They were brought into the Central Committee together when Lenin needed to inject some 'roughness'. He worked closely with Stalin during the Civil War. As leader of the Caucasus region, he brutally ended Georgian independence. Ordzhonikidze supported Stalin in the power-struggle and was rewarded with a seat in the Politburo. After 1930, he led the drive to build up heavy industry. He supported high targets but quarrelled with Molotov over methods and the use of non-Communist specialists. He committed suicide to avoid arrest.

Valerian KUIBYSHEV *1883–1935*

Stalin's other Deputy Secretary, Kuibyshev had been with the Party since 1904 and joined the Politburo in 1927. After helping Stalin in the power-struggle, he took over the Supreme Economic Council. Here he led the attack on NEP and the drive for rapid industrialisation. He moved on to run Gosplan, and drew up the first Five Year Plan. He is said to have been among those who called for a more moderate policy in the mid-1930s although this is not clear. He apparently died naturally although the police boss, Yagoda, confessed later to his murder.

Sergei KIROV *1886–1934*

A Bolshevik activist since 1906, he was a leader of the Revolution in Siberia. He fought alongside Stalin in the Civil War and worked with him in Georgia. In 1925 he took over Leningrad from Zinoviev and played a leading role in defeating Stalin's opponents there. In the Politburo from 1930, he was a popular leader in the Party who many saw as Stalin's eventual successor. It is unclear whether he opposed Stalin in 1932–3 and his assassination in 1934 remains a mystery.

Lazar KAGANOVICH *1893–1991?*

Kaganovich is perhaps the archetypal Stalinist: a ruthless organiser with a reputation for getting things done. A Bolshevik from 1911, he became Secretary of the Ukraine Party in 1925 and purged it of Stalin's opponents. A leader of the Collectivisation Campaign, he also played a leading role in the Party Purges. As industrial trouble-shooter Kaganovich was given control of transport, which he ran until 1944. Despite fading from power in the 1940s and being a Jew, he survived well into his 90s.

Andrei ZHDANOV *1896–1948*

An agitator in the Revolutionary Army, he rose to prominence as a Party Organiser and was one of the architects of 'Socialist Realism' in the arts. He took over and purged Leningrad after Kirov's death. He led the campaign for party democracy which contributed to the 'Terror', although he quarrelled with police boss Ezhov about the Party Purges. A strong Nationalist, Zhdanov was political leader of Leningrad during the seige and led the attack on alien elements in the arts after the War. Regarded as a possible successor to Stalin, his stature is indicated by the brutal purge of his supporters carried out after his premature death. Stalin was always convinced he had been murdered.

Stalinist leaders in 1934 (left to right, back) Enukidze, Voroshilov, Kaganovich, Kuibyshev; (front) Ordzhonikidze, Stalin, Molotov, Kirov

PART TWO

CHAPTER ONE

A GREY BLUR? UNDERSTANDING THE RISE OF STALIN

Objectives

◢ To understand why Stalin became dictator of the USSR by 1929
◢ To decide if this represented a break with the past

1879	Joseph Djugashvili born in Gori, Georgia
1898	After expulsion from his Jesuit Seminary (religious school) he becomes a Revolutionary
1904	Member of the tiny Bolshevik wing of the Social Democratic (Marxist) Party
1912	Lenin appoints him to Central Committee of Party
1917	Helps organise Bolsheviks prior to Lenin's return
1922	Party General Secretary
1924	One of the Collective Leadership after Lenin
1929	Sole leader

To many on the Left, the tragedy of the Russian Revolution was that Stalin, rather than Trotsky, succeeded Lenin as leader. Many in the West were not surprised that a Communist regime, imposed on Russia by force, resulted in Stalin's 'totalitarian' regime. Yet in 1924, Stalin did not appear a likely successor. Sukhanov's characterisation of him as a 'grey blur' captures his rather anonymous, bureaucratic profile. Lenin himself had given instructions for his removal. How was it that in five years he had outmanoeuvred more fancied candidates to succeed? Any response to this question requires an understanding of the developments, debates and divisions within the Communist Party after 1921, and the way the leading figures related to them.

Lenin's legacy

The Civil War had a radical effect on the Communists and forced Lenin to adapt Marxist ideas to ensure survival. In 1918 they only controlled some major cities and industrial areas. Most of Russia was beyond anyone's control as peasants seized the land. Faced with internal enemies, foreign invasion and economic collapse, Lenin forced his reluctant colleagues to accept a series of pragmatic compromises.

◢ To gain breathing space, Lenin bought off Germany in 1918 and Poland in 1921 with territory. This was a retreat from the Marxist goal of spreading revolutionary war to Europe.

◢ The Red Army was organised by Trotsky on traditional lines and retained many ex-Tsarist officers. Discipline was strict. This upset idealists who wanted a partisan army without ranks and orders.

◢ To ensure supplies reached the Army, workers were not allowed to control the economy. Under **War Communism**, capitalist managers were retained and discipline imposed on workers and trade unions. A Supreme Economic Council (SEC) was set up under FELIX DZERZHINSKI to control the economy.

Profile FELIX DZERZHINSKI 1877–1926

Dzerzhinski had been a Bolshevik since 1902. He was an intellectual, hardened by over 15 years of imprisonment. He helped to organise the October Revolution and had many key posts in Lenin's governments. He organised the Bolshevik Terror against their opponents and later took responsibility for overseeing transport and economic development. Stalin later hijacked his nickname as 'the great industrialiser'. Fiercely loyal to the Party and viewed as incorruptible, it is unlikely that Stalin could have succeeded so completely had he lived. He died suddenly of a heart attack in 1926, for which some suspected his successor at the NKVD (Menzhinski) of poisoning him.

◢ When Army and workers ran out of food, requisition squads seized grain from the peasants. This triggered a brutal, rural civil war. Food was rationed according to individuals' value in the struggle.

◢ Political opposition was met with 'Terror'. Dzerzhinski organised the CHEKA (Secret Police) to destroy counter-revolutionaries and to shoot deserters. After the Civil War its name was changed to OGPU as part of the Interior Ministry (NKVD).

◢ Food shortages and harsh central control led to discontent. Some left-wing critics (called democratic centralisers) had demanded greater democracy. Others, known as the 'Workers' Opposition', wanted greater workers' rights. Similar demands were made by the Kronstadt mutineers in 1921. To preserve unity, Lenin suppressed divisions in the Party. The Red Army crushed the mutiny and persistent dissidents were expelled from the Party. Lenin demanded 'Iron Discipline'.

◢ In 1921, to relieve famine and avert economic collapse, Lenin abandoned War Communism. His *New Economic Policy (NEP)* made many concessions to the peasants and restored small-scale capitalism to revitalise production and trade in food and consumer goods.

Key Term

The New Economic Policy (NEP) was Lenin's pragmatic response to the Kronstadt mutiny, peasant unrest and economic collapse. It allowed peasants to sell surplus grain at a profit in return for payment of tax. Small-scale industry was returned to private control and traders or 'Nepmen' encouraged to re-open markets to connect town and countryside (see chapter 2).

◢ Lenin had promised self-determination to the non-Russian nations of the Tsarist Empire. After the Civil War, when world revolution had not occurred, he persuaded breakaway republics into the new federation (the USSR).

By 1922 Lenin was ill from an attempted assassination and strokes. He died early in 1924. He had held the Party together, inspiring it to seize and hold power. He left no strategy for development or a successor of his calibre. In this vacuum, the power-struggle developed.

Stalin's rise

In 1912 Lenin promoted Djugashvili and fellow Georgian, Ordzonikidze, because he wanted some rougher 'men of the people' to balance his westernised intellectuals. Djugashvili's nickname, Stalin, means 'man of steel'. 'Stalin' played a minor role in the October Revolution but his ruthlessness made him useful as a political comm-issar in the Civil War. During this time he and his close colleagues (Ordzhonikidze, Voroshilov and Budyenny) frequently clashed with Trotsky. His loyalty was rewarded with a series of key posts, including

Commissar for Nationalities. In this role, he persuaded the Non-Russian Republics into the new USSR, using force where necessary. Lenin considered dismissing him after the way he and Ordzhonikidze overthrew the Menshevik government of Georgia.

Stalin also held key roles in the Party. Lenin's great organiser, Yakov Sverdlov (who died in 1919), proved impossible to replace. In 1922 a Secretariat was set up under Stalin who proved adept at administration and was soon on all the key committees. His job included keeping party records, appointing Communist officials, settling disputes, removing those who didn't follow the Moscow line and controlling links with the regions. He appointed to over 1,000 posts in his first year. Some of his associates became Secretaries of the Republics: Kirov in Azerbaijan, Molotov in the Ukraine and Kaganovich in Turkestan.

Stalin was secretive and conspiratorial, and renowned for his memory, shrewdness and timing. He was also known as ruthless and vengeful. Lenin criticised his 'roughness' and his 'Russian chauvinism'. Retained because of his loyalty and practical ability, he disturbed other leaders with his growing power in the Party bureaucracy (see Figure 5).

The Communist Party in the 1920s

Lenin had originally intended that after a brief period the workers would govern themselves. However, they lacked expertise and knowledge of Marxism, so the Party continued to run the USSR on their behalf. By the mid-1920s, Government and Party were inseparable.

After Lenin's purge of his leftist critics, there was an attempt to attract new recruits to the Party. As numbers grew from around 472,000 in 1924 to 1.3 million in 1928, the original Bolsheviks and civil war veterans were swamped by newcomers. The newcomers were different in other respects (as the tables in Figure 6 show).

While leading positions in 1924 were held by Revolutionary Veterans, they were in a minority below the Central Committee level. The Party remained largely male. Women increased but as many leading female Bolsheviks had been on the Left they held few prominent positions. The new Party was young, inexperienced and poorly educated; less than 8% had been to secondary school.

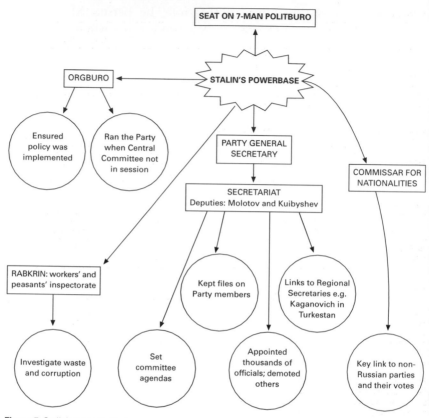

Figure 5 Stalin's power in the bureaucracy

The Party did not hold all the official posts. Due to the shortage of educated members, only about 20 per cent of state employees were Communists and only 5 per cent of the Supreme Economic Council. In rural areas there were only 200,000 members in a population of 120 million. Non-Party representatives dominated rural soviets. These factors sowed the seeds of the internal Party problems of the 1930s. How do you control such a Party? Do you use education or tough discipline?

Party debates

The Communists hoped to remain in power to build an industrial socialist society despite foreign hostility. There were many divisions over how to achieve this.

1 Social origin (%)

	Workers	Peasants	White collar	Other (intellectual *etc.*)
1919	52.0	15.0	18.0	14.0
1923	43.0	26.0	29.0	
1928	56.5	22.9	18.3	2.0

* Note: this data may be suspect as members sought to conceal bourgeois origins and the Party sought to demonstrate its proletarian nature.

2 Ethnic origin (%) [brackets give % of the whole population]

	Russian	Jewish	Turko-Tatar	Ukrainian
1924	60.8 [53]	11.3	1.0 [11]	4.7 [21]
1927	62.0	c 9.4	1.6	9.8

3 Actual Jobs (%)

	Workers (incl. managers)	Government officials	Red Army	Peasants	Kulaks or managers	Other (incl. Party officials)
1919	11.0	53.0	27.0			8.0
1928	35.2	38.3	6.3	12.0	9.2	9.8

4 Age and sex (%)

	Men < 30	Men < 40	Women
1919	50	90	7.5 (1922)
1928	50	85	12.8

5 Percentage of positions held by those who joined pre-1917

Politburo	100
Central Committee	92
Senior Secretaries	71 (+14% veterans)
Party delegates	44
Members	1.4

Figure 6 The membership of the Communist Party

Now that the Civil War was won, allow non-Bolshevik Socialists (fellow travellers) to help rebuild Russia. **Nikolai Bukharin**	*Preserve the CP's monopoly of power as the true proletarian organisation. Beware of class enemies.* **Josef Stalin**
Impose military discipline to achieve a rapid transformation. **Leon Trotsky**	*Give more of a role to the trade unions.* **Mikhail Tomsky**
Squeeze the peasants to provide investment capital for rapid industrialisation. **Preobrazhenski, Trotsky** and later **Dzerzhinski**	*Continue with NEP. Work to convert the peasants to Socialism. Gradually develop the links between town and farms (*Smychka*).* **Bukharin**

Spread class conflict abroad to divide and destabilise capitalist countries. This 'Permanent Revolution' would achieve security for the USSR in the long term. **Trotsky** and **Zinoviev**	Rely on Soviet strength to develop Communism in the USSR and provide security ('Socialism in one country'). **Bukharin, Alexei Rykov** and **Stalin**

The power-struggle: events

Act 1: 1922–4

Stalin was out of favour with Lenin but Trotsky ignored Lenin's request to attack his style and power and Zinoviev and Kamenev protected Stalin as they feared Trotsky. They also refused to publish Lenin's *Testament* because it embarrassed each of them.

The Politburo in 1924 consisted of TROTSKY, Zinoviev, Kamenev, Stalin, Bukharin, Rykov and Tomsky. Trotsky would have won an open election but decisions were made by the Party Congress and Trotsky did not hold a major Party post. His rivals portrayed his attack on NEP as disloyal and his call for greater democracy as a bid for power. The others feared him and isolated him in voting. Rebuffed and ill, he retired to the Caucasus and missed Lenin's funeral. He claimed Stalin gave him the wrong date! When he returned, his call for permanent revolution was dismissed as 'warmongering', showing a lack of faith in the USSR.

Profile 'TROTSKY'; LEV BRONSTEIN 1879–1940

He was a Jewish, Marxist intellectual who had led the Petrograd Soviet in 1905. He joined the Bolsheviks from the Mensheviks in 1917, in time to organise the October Revolution. He then organised the Red Army and led it to victory in the Civil War. A charismatic speaker, Trotsky was widely expected to succeed Lenin but was outmanoeuvred and expelled from Russia. In exile, he continued to oppose Stalin until his murder in Mexico in 1940. His brand of Marxism has proved more influential in the West than Stalin's.

Stalin gave Lenin a state funeral against the wishes of his widow Krupskaya and embalmed his body in a mausoleum in Red Square. Petrograd was renamed Leningrad. With his lectures on the 'Foundations of Leninism', Stalin presented Lenin's works in a way ordinary people could understand and which made Trotsky look bad. This 'cult of Lenin' also boosted Stalin's profile as his master's humble comrade. From now on, leaders quoted Lenin to support their policies.

◢ Source

The party must stand at the head of the working class, it must see further than the working class: it must lead the proletariat, and not follow the tail . . . The dictatorship of the proletariat is impossible without a party which is strong . . . the existence of factions is incompatible either with the Party's unity or with its iron discipline. The Party becomes strong by purging itself of opportunist elements.

Josef Stalin, **The Foundations of Leninism** *(1924)*

Zinoviev led the increasingly personal attacks on Trotsky emphasizing his Menshevik origins. Faced with hostile Congresses, Trotsky gave up and retired from commanding the Army to demonstrate that he was not plotting a coup. Some writers think he felt the struggle for personal power was beneath him.

Act 2: 1924–6

Zinoviev and Kamenev became increasingly concerned about Stalin's power. They were also Party bosses in Leningrad and Moscow, where new grain shortages threatened order. However, when they launched an attack on NEP and 'Socialism in One Country', Rykov (president) and Tomsky (trade unions) backed Bukharin and Stalin. This gave the **'Rightists'** a 4 : 3 majority in the Politburo but Stalin's connections also ensured a clear majority in the Party Congress.

After crushing Zinoviev and Kamenev at the 1925 Party Congress, Stalin removed their power-bases. Kirov took over Leningrad and the Moscow Party was cleared of their supporters. During 1926 the Politburo was enlarged with Stalin's allies Molotov, Voroshilov, Kuibyshev and Rudzutak. Stalin could also usually rely on Kalinin. Ethnic differences became important. Many **'Leftists'** had been Jews, the Right largely Russians. Many of Stalin's group were from the Caucasus.

The Right appeared strong with support in the Commissariats (*e.g.* Agriculture) and the State Organisations (*e.g.* Gosplan, State Bank). Loyal Dzerzhinski headed both Supreme Economic Council and OGPU. Bukharin may have thought of ousting Stalin in 1925 and replacing him with Dzerzhinski but chose to avoid splitting the Party. When Dzerzhinski died in 1926, two Stalinists – Kuibyshev and Menzhinski – replaced him.

Act 3: 1926–7

Too late, the 'Leftists' – Kamenev, Trotsky and Zinoviev – teamed up as the 'United Opposition' but had lost both credibility and support and were voted from the Politburo and other offices. Their supporters were hounded from posts by the OGPU. Amid economic problems and war scares, Stalin put aside calls from the 'Rightists' to be lenient. In 1927 the 'Leftists' were expelled from the Party and in 1929 Trotsky was deported.

KEY TERMS

Leftists and **Rightists** were labels applied by Stalin to his opponents. 'Leftists' included Trotsky, Kamenev, Zinoviev and Preobrazhenski. They were associated with rapid industrialisation (Bukharin called them 'Superindustrialists'), anti-peasant policies, greater democracy in the Party and spreading revolution. 'Rightists' included Bukharin, Rykov, Tomsky and possibly Genrikh Yagoda. They are associated with a gradual path to Socialism via NEP and good relations between workers and peasants. Stalin was considered a 'Rightist' until 1928.

Trotsky had accused Stalin of setting bureaucracy over the people. Bureaucracy was the key to Stalin's victories as he used the support of Party bosses to smash each successive challenge. A pattern was set in which opposition criticised the leadership, was accused of faction or counter-revolution and purged. By late 1927 the Right were worried. Bukharin made an attempt to link with Kamenev, but failed.

Act 4: 1928–9

Stalin and his supporters demanded that collectivisation and rapid industrialisation replace NEP. They attacked non-party experts and called for a militant line in the **Comintern**.

Kuibyshev demanded a squeeze of the **kulaks** to fund industrial investment. The Right defended NEP and criticised Party bureaucracy. Again there was a race for support in the Party Committees and Congress. The Right dominated many of the government organisations and the trade unions, but Stalin had a majority where it counted. Party bosses, worried about peasant unrest, supported him. He was also supported by delegates from the non-Russian Republics, who owed their positions to the Commissar for Nationalities. Stalin used their votes to sweep his opponents aside. By December it was over. 'Rightists' were branded a pro-kulak deviation and removed from office. It was impossible to be a loyal opposition.

KEY TERMS

Comintern – the International Communist movement – was set up by Lenin to help spread revolution abroad. Initially led by Zinoviev, it seemed to fail in its early years. Stalin purged it and brought it under tight Moscow control. It generally operated in the interests of Soviet, rather than world, Communism.

Kulaks were the better-off peasants. It is rather a 'blanket term' and some writers have questioned whether they really existed. However, most Communists believed they did and that they were hoarding grain during the difficult years of NEP.

Bukharin did criticise Stalin's new policies, but only within closed Party meetings. Party secrecy meant that Bukharin was unable to mobilise the support he had in the country. This support is evident in the scale of Stalin's expulsion of 'Rightists': 78–85 per cent of members of the Factory Committees in Moscow, Leningrad, Urals and Ukraine were replaced and 11 per cent of the entire Party were expelled. As Trotsky had predicted, political life was choked off. There were still Party barons, such as Kirov in Leningrad and Ordzhonikidze in Trancaucasia, but in 1929 they preferred Stalin's action to Bukharin's patience. Finally, in December, the Rightists 'confessed' their errors. Probably to save friends from arrest and to preserve party unity.

Historical explanations

The events of Stalin's rise to power are well known and generally agreed on. The reasons for it are subject to debate. Historians have constructed differing accounts from broadly similar evidence because they attribute different value to pieces of evidence and varying significance to key factors. In the case of Stalin, there are also political and historical factors which particularly limit the reliability of the evidence. Reasons for this will be explored in later chapters.

A number of broad approaches can be distinguished. (Examples of historians who have put forward these ideas are given in brackets.)

◢ Structuralist explanations

Stalin and his regime were the product of the system and their times, not the other way round. Marx would probably agree with this. We have not experienced in the West the disastrous combination of civil war, famine, invasion and ruin in which Russia found itself. A strong state and a leader with energy and ruthlessness who could mobilise the masses to avoid disaster was required. Given the recent economic and political development of Russia, this was also more likely. (Von Laue)

Some writers have fitted Stalin into the Russian tradition of absolute rulers. He was a 'red Tsar' who recognised that Russia was not the West and that state power and political police could be progressive in reshaping the Russian people in order to meet foreign threats. Lenin feared this 'Russification' of the revolution, but there is evidence that Stalin viewed it more positively.

◢ Stalin was the product of Lenin and Communism

This was a popular view in the West. Lenin set up a centralised state and secret police. He organised the Party on bureaucratic lines, purged it of dissidents and used 'Terror' against his enemies. Dictatorship leads to despotism, or so the logic goes. However, Lenin didn't shoot his colleagues. (Leonard Shapiro and Robert Conquest)

◢ Stalin was lucky

A series of accidents – including the deaths of Sverdlov, Lenin and Dzerzhinski – assisted Stalin's rise. Lenin's ban on faction and the restriction of the struggle to the Party played into his hands. His opponents all made serious errors. Stalin twice offered to resign but this was not accepted. There was an alternative strategy available with Bukharin and the continuation of NEP, but the Party lost its nerve. (Stephen Cohen and Read)

◢ *Stalin was mad, evil or ruthless*

This is a popular explanation for why any leading figure was different to ourselves. We can always find some motive in a person's childhood and this sort of psychoanalytical interpretation can be attractive. Robert Tucker discusses Stalin's delusions of hidden enemies, his idealisation of himself as revolutionary hero and vindictiveness towards those who denied him.

◢ Source

Power for power's own sake was never his aim. His life in politics was a never-ending endeavour to prove himself a revolutionary hero as Lenin did before him, and receive, as Lenin did before him, the plaudits of a grateful party for his exploits as leader. Power was a prime means to Stalin's supreme goal: fame and glory.

Robert Tucker, **Stalin in Power** (Norton, 1992)

Others have commented on Stalin's height (5 ft 4 in/1.6 m) and tendency to be a loner. Certainly he killed his colleagues and executions declined after his death, but even if this approach identifies underlying drives it cannot explain why he succeeded. Many have these 'traits', but they don't all become dictators. Some detect a pure power lust in Stalin, yet the Marxist group he joined in 1898 were political no-hopers.

◢ Source

The experience of the first half of his life, living on the margins of society, often in the company of thieves ... left psychological handicaps from which he was never able to free himself. He emerged as a rough, coarse man whose original motivation as a revolutionary was coloured far more by hatred and resentment than by idealism ... believing that 'well organised violence was the shortest route between two points'.

Alan Bullock, **Hitler and Stalin** (HarperCollins, 1991)

◢ *Stalin was a clever politician*

This is another approach which focuses on Stalin as the key element. Trotsky depicted Stalin as a mediocrity, a dull Georgian with no distinctive policies. He certainly accepted unglamorous posts which no

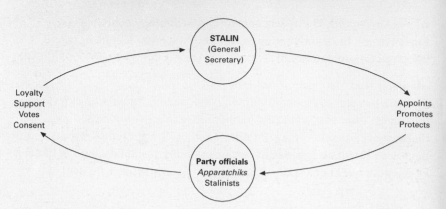

Figure 7 The circular flow of power

one foresaw as the source of future power. Stalin built up the rickety state structure and used it. As a 'machine politician' he was able to transfer or demote opponents while promoting his networks of supporters. He created a circular flow of power (see Figure 7). He also used the policy debates to further his position; often appearing as a mediator while magnifying the differences between others. Instinctively on the Left, he concealed this until his rivals had destroyed each other. (Moshe Lewin, E H Carr and Graeme Gill)

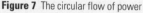 *Stalin was in tune with the Party*

Stalin, with his peasant origins and toughness, contrasted with the rival westernised intellectuals. While they wrote academic treatises, he simplified Lenin for the masses. It isn't clear if Stalin even read much Marx. His social conservatism, distaste for NEP and even his anti-semitism would have been close to the ideas of the silent majority in the Party. A good listener to the Party, he was able to turn the self-preservation of officials, fearful of attacks on bureaucracy, to his advantage. His Red-Russian patriotism seemed to offer a new form of identity which even non-Russians could share. After years of upheaval he offered stability, while his authoritarian nature played well to men militarised by the Civil War.

◢ Source

Intrigue, treachery and terror also contributed to his success, but by themselves they do not account for Stalin's extraordinary role or popularity.

   *Norman Pereira, 'Stalin and the Communist Party in the 1920s', **History Today** (1992)*

1 Make two lists of the strengths and weaknesses of each position from the evidence you have.
2 Write an essay: 'Why did Stalin become Soviet leader by 1929?' (This is one of the most common types of question at A-Level and focuses on causation.)

Handy tips

In deciding what to include you should try to:

◢ demonstrate an awareness of the order of events and key characters
◢ focus mainly on possible reasons for his rise
◢ use your knowledge to evaluate the possible reasons
◢ show an awareness of the limitations of the evidence available
◢ demonstrate an understanding of why historians have reached the verdicts they have
◢ come to your own conclusions on the basis of these.

In writing up your essay:

◢ Address the question or set the scene in the introduction.
◢ Use each paragraph to develop one clear, relevant idea or interpretation. The broad explanations provide you with possible headings.
◢ Use the past tense.
◢ Use detail *sparingly* (including short quotations) to support your judgements.
◢ Draw your ideas together and sum up your judgement in the conclusion.

The most common errors made by students with this type of question are:

◢ irrelevance (long descriptions of the Revolution or the 1930s)
◢ narrative. Even if the question contains the word 'how', you will rarely get much above half marks for even a good *description* of Stalin's rise.

CHAPTER TWO

THE 'REVOLUTION FROM ABOVE'?: ECONOMIC CHANGE 1926–30

The NEP

From 1921–28, the Soviet economy was run on the basis of Lenin's New Economic Policy (NEP). After 1928 there was a dramatic change towards rapid industrialisation and the forced collectivisation of the peasantry. Since this coincided with Stalin's defeat of Bukharin and the Right and a series of major social and cultural changes, many historians call these changes a 'second revolution'. Typical accounts have Stalin imposing revolutionary changes from above, either to safeguard his personal power or to strengthen the USSR to withstand invasion.

In order to evaluate these views, we need to ask:
◢ **How critical were the problems facing the USSR in the late 1920s?**
◢ **Did NEP fail or was it destroyed?**
◢ **Did Stalin have a coherent plan which he carried through?**
◢ **Why was collectivisation so rapid and so violent?**

The key to resolving these questions lies in grasping the order of events in the late 1920s and understanding the range of causes at work. Diagrams are more useful than notes in enabling you to capture complex situations. For this particular issue a flow diagram would be appropriate (see Figures 8 and 9 on page 38). Try task 1 on page 57.

NEP agriculture

NEP began as a concession to the peasants and it is important to grasp their critical importance in the economy in order to understand what came later. Grain was the most vital resource in the Soviet economy. The basic element in the diet of the population, it was also the principal means of earning foreign income and thus paying for industrial investment. Development depended on successful grain harvests.

Most peasants were little more than subsistence farmers. Large-scale farmers who produced for urban markets had been eliminated in the revolution, leaving narrow divisions of wealth between rich and poor peasants. Most were prepared to sell surplus grain for high prices; but when prices were low, farmers simply consumed more or used the extra to fatten their animals since produce such as meat, cheese and leather could be sold on the open market. Nevertheless, more commercial attitudes were emerging. Over 6 million households joined marketing or credit cooperatives and some grew richer by producing extra for market or by hiring out equipment. Some were able to hire labourers. Whether this made them a genuine *kulak* class is debatable.

Industry
The USSR inherited a relatively narrow range of industries which were devastated after eight years of conflict. Most industry was nationalised, with the state appointing managers to run it. Often these managers were not Communists. Less than 1 per cent of large-scale industry remained in private hands by the late 1920s and private enterprises employed less than 1 per cent of all workers.

Consolidation
The New Economic Policy's first task was to return the economy to its prewar level. This was largely accomplished by 1925, mainly by restoring damaged plants to full capacity.
- Coal and oil production had surpassed 1913 levels.
- Chemicals, electricity and engineering had all grown.
- Iron and steel production, devastated in the civil war, still lagged behind. Crisis was avoided, however, partly because of reduced demand for arms, ships, rails and so on.
- Peasants produced sufficient food for the urban markets but insufficient for the state to export to buy industrial equipment.
- Food processing lagged well behind prewar levels.

Dilemma: which path to industrialisation?

Lenin defined Communism as 'Electrification plus Soviet Power'. His ideal was a Socialist version of the USA; but Marx had not provided him with a blueprint to get there. Lenin pessimistically warned that people over 50 would not live to see Socialism, although those under 15 would. Faced with a hostile world and aware of their feeble arms industries, the USSR also needed a steel and machine making capability for defence. The Communists' task was to learn state capitalism from the Germans and management from America while enlarging the working class to provide political support.

Paying for widespread industrialisation and mechanisation was the key problem. Tsarist industrialisation had been financed by exploiting the peasants and was dominated by foreign capitalists. These capitalists were gone and since the Bolsheviks had repudiated foreign debts, they were unlikely to lend them any more money. The USSR had to move from one non-capitalist economic system to a new one, but with little gold or foreign currency. Difficult decisions had to be made:

1 Should they improve agriculture first, or invest in industry?

2 What should take priority: consumer goods or heavy industry?

3 Should they import tractors, or machinery to build their own?

4 Should there be total central control or still a role for the market?

5 What were the risks and how much time did they have?

By the mid-1920s, two rival Communist models were on offer:
◢ 'primitive Socialist accumulation'
◢ 'moving towards Socialism at the speed of the peasant nag'.

Profile EVGENY PREOBRAZHENSKI 1886–1937

Preobrazhenski was a long-time Bolshevik from Eastern Russia, prominent in the Revolution in Siberia and on the 'Leftist' wing of the Party. He campaigned for democracy in the Party and rapid industrialisation, both of which led to clashes with Lenin. His economic theories underpinned attacks on NEP and were those Bukharin had to answer. He also sided with Trotsky and Zinoviev in the power-struggle which led to his expulsion from the Party. Ironically, Stalin then used many of his ideas. He reappeared for the 1936 Moscow Trials and was executed the following year.

1 'Primitive Socialist accumulation'

PREOBRAZHENSKI wanted to tax the peasants heavily and keep goods prices high to reduce consumption of scarce resources. 'Leftist' advocates of this line believed that industrialisation was the priority. They wanted to buy peasant grain cheaply and sell it abroad to provide investment capital. Trotsky wanted something similar although he believed that it was impossible for Russia to industrialise without foreign help. He saw NEP as a temporary halt which risked the decay of both Party and Socialism unless it was replaced. After the defeat of the Left in the power-struggle, these ideas were declared contrary to the Party general line.

2 'Moving towards Socialism at the speed of the peasant nag'

Bukharin responded by developing NEP as a Socialist theory with identical goals to Preobrazhenski's but his methods were more moderate.

- Encourage trade between peasants and towns to thrive (**Smychka**).

- By gradually adjusting prices in favour of the towns, accumulate surplus capital to finance a move towards Socialism, 'at the speed of the peasant nag'.

- Instead of exploiting the peasants like parasitic capitalists, Communists should educate and win them over to ideals of cooperation and collectivisation.

Bukharin called his rivals 'superindustrialists' and claimed their anti-peasant policy would lead to conflict which might threaten the regime. The immediate task was to restore consumer demand and ensure a supply of goods. Once prices were reduced, peasants would sell more grain, so more could be invested.

Under Bukharin and Stalin, this policy became the general party line.

KEY TERM

Smychka was the key to NEP. It was the ratio between the prices of grain and consumer goods. Prices had to be at a level which would persuade the peasants to sell grain while also giving the towns a profit through sales of goods to the peasants. If grain prices were too high, then peasants wouldn't grow industrial crops such as beet. If they were too low, then they wouldn't provide sufficient food for the towns. The towns had to do better than the peasants from this in order for the State to build up a surplus for industrial investment. This delicate relationship, or 'Smychka', faced the added complication that while the State bought over 50% of the grain it did not have a monopoly. Private merchants could also trade in grain so the State had to match their prices.

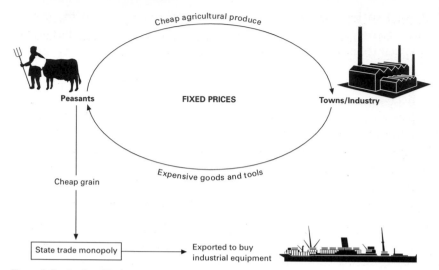

Figure 8 Preobrazhenski's theory: a massive transfer of resources from agriculture to industry to enable rapid investment to address backwardness

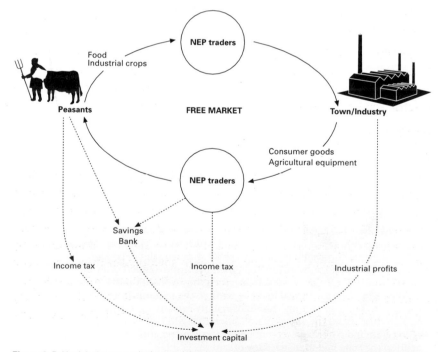

Figure 9 Bukharin's theory: gradual, natural development by stimulating both sectors (*Smychka*)

A command economy

The Party was in agreement that the State should lead industrialisation. Two key organisations were responsible for this.

1 The Supreme Economic Council (*Vesenkha*) was responsible for decision-making and overseeing the economy. Under Felix Dzerzhinski, the Supreme Economic Council had supervised the rebuilding of Russian industry. After his death in 1926, Stalin appointed Valerian Kuibyshev who demanded more rapid investment. Kuibyshev argued that since Russia's ability to finance imports of technology depended upon the fickle agricultural sector, they needed to squeeze more resources from the peasantry.

2 Gosplan (the State planning agency) had been established in 1921 to provide projections and to collect statistical data on economic performance. In 1926 its largely non-Bolshevik economists produced a general plan for growth. This was gradual, being constrained by economic realities. Vesenkha put forward rival, more extravagant plans which put more faith in energy and party enthusiasm. There followed two years of bitter debate.

Meanwhile, the Party decided on a moderate increase in industrial investment, cutting administrative costs to finance it. Among the major infrastructure projects commissioned was a massive hydro-electric scheme on the Dnieper river.

Problems

Prices

In 1924, NEP ran into the 'scissors crisis' where grain prices had fallen while goods prices had risen so peasants had not provided sufficient grain. Disaster had been averted by concessions to the peasants at the expense of industry. In 1925, Bukharin appealed to peasants to 'enrich yourselves' (a phrase he later regretted) and slashed grain taxes by 25 per cent. Zinoviev, Kamenev and Lenin's widow Krupskaya attacked this as '*kulak* deviation' and forecast that rich peasants would hold the country to ransom. They thought the government should rely solely on the poorer peasants and workers. Stalin ensured that the Party supported Bukharin's line.

Productivity

Output per worker rose slowly as industry moved towards larger units, standardised production lines and the use of shift work. It remained low by international standards. In the state sector they attempted to adopt American management techniques like 'Taylorist' ideas of scientific management which involved experts dividing jobs into simple component tasks and working out the quickest ways of doing them. Workers would then be paid on piece-rate, which enabled wage rises to be kept below productivity gains. Instead of representing workers against management, trade unions were held responsible for the productivity of their members. When strikes did occur they were largely 'unofficial'. Nevertheless, labour discipline and efficiency remained poor.

Political unease

The Party never really got used to NEP. Many Communists were disturbed at the approval for NEP shown by their former enemies. About one in ten shopfloor workers were Party members by 1928 and many workers resented key aspects of NEP, such as the concessions to the peasants and privileges given to experts (often bourgeois in origin) above them. Most NEP 'capitalists' (or 'Nepmen') did not own premises and the bulk were market traders or self-employed artisans (skilled workers) rather than manufacturers. They were taxed at 50% and frequently suffered harassment by officials, such as withdrawal of licences. They provided a convenient scapegoat for high prices and shortages. NEP itself didn't look like a proletarian revolution and was portrayed as capitalistic or pre-revolutionary 'degeneration'. Stalin would tap this resentment, but until then NEP remained the general line.

1927: the crisis of NEP

Despite the successful 1926 grain harvest, State procurements (collections) were only half of what was expected. The government blamed '*kulak* speculators' and responded by raising taxes on richer peasants to force them to sell, while introducing penalties for hoarding grain.

The problem was that grain was being produced but not reaching markets. It wasn't worth the peasants selling it, since there were insufficient consumer goods for them to buy – so they consumed it instead. It also reflected levelling within the peasantry. Before 1914, most of the State's grain had come from large estates. By 1926, 85% came from middling or poorer farmers who sent proportionally less to market anyway – only 13% of the harvest being sold compared with 26% prewar. Large numbers keeping a little back had a massive knock-on effect.

To deal with this crisis, a series of measures were taken. They triggered a chain of events which, linked with the power-struggle going on simultaneously, destroyed NEP.

1 To induce peasants to sell grain to buy goods, retail prices were cut. This backfired. Townspeople snapped up available goods (candles, crockery, soap, matches and so on), thus leaving less for the villagers. Chronic goods shortages were exacerbated by the policy shift towards investment in heavy industry which diverted resources away from consumer industries.

2 Fearing another 'scissors crisis', OGPU moved against 'speculators' during 1927; harassing and rounding up Nepmen. Licences were withdrawn and markets broken up, while some police (illegally) seized grain 'surpluses'. Private trading began to be viewed by hard-liners in the Party as a 'black market'.

3 In early 1927, the Party was united behind the clampdown on speculators and in establishing some trial collectivisation projects in the Urals. Requisition (*zagotovki*) was instituted in place of grain sales, but peasants had to be paid the market price for grain taken. Molotov, Stalin's ally, warned that force should not be used as it would be against the people and would threaten the *Smychka*.

4 For the 1927 harvest, grain prices were reduced; but after initial success, deliveries fell again. This jeopardised industrialisation and food supplies for the urban workforce. Recent studies of harvest patterns suggest that this fall in yield was due to the weather, but the Party at the time believed *kulaks* were withholding grain.

5 The leadership now divided over how to address this crisis.
    ◢ On the Right, Bukharin, Kalinin and Rykov wanted to complete existing projects and limit investment until they could afford it. They believed that the countryside was not ready for

Communism yet, so the *Smychka* should be preserved and price controls, not police action, should be their key tools.

◢ Stalin, Molotov and Kuibyshev wanted more rapid industrialisation. They began to use the language of class war but had not yet developed an alternative to NEP. The split was over pace, methods and priorities: coercion or flexibility. Stalin's supporters used a war scare in the Far East to support their line.

6 The Fifteenth Party Congress in December 1927 is when Stalin revealed his change of heart, and was later called the 'Collectivisation Congress'. Yet other options were discussed. Proposals for an agricultural Five Year Plan still assumed a dominant private sector and did not propose liquidation of the *kulaks*. Collective farms were to be built up gradually, to compete with private peasants to force them to sell their surplus. Even when agricultural plans were ratified in May 1929 there was no reference to seizing animals or mass collectivisation. Collectivisation was to be voluntary and its speed related to the ability of industry to provide machinery.

1928: Stalin's left-turn

1928 saw Stalin's political victory over the 'Rightists'.

1 During January, grain shortages led to emergency measures against *kulak* speculators. Stalin toured Siberia demanding greater efforts from officials. He ordered them to find more grain and to pay lower prices. After procuring the grain, Stalin advocated the application of these 'Urals–Siberian methods', which involved emergency 'contracts', requisition and the use of force because 'so long as there are *kulaks*, so long will there be sabotage of grain procurements'.

2 Stalin's demands coincided with a wider campaign against 'wreckers' which would culminate in the Show Trials. Private merchants were increasingly harassed and Party Officials in Smolensk were expelled following an investigation by *Rabkrin* (Workers' and Peasants' Inspectorate), which was dominated by Stalinists. Their crime was allowing *kulaks* and other 'degenerates' to take over the 'Red Land Improver', a showpiece collective farm. Other officials recognised this as a warning to be 'vigilant'.

3 Unity finally collapsed at the July 1928 Central Committee meeting where Bukharin called for balanced development based on the *Smychka*, while Stalin demanded cheap grain to fund the Five Year Plan. Bukharin compared Stalin to Genghis Khan and predicted that his proposals would cause such conflict that the Party would have to 'drown the risings in blood'. Bukharin favoured importing grain rather than war with the peasants. To Stalin's group, this was defeatist. For the final time, the Committee backed Bukharin. It was the last occasion of open discussion in the Party.

4 After this, Stalin really began campaigning against the Right. Ordzonikidze and Kuibyshev proposed speeding up industrialisation, ignoring Rightist fears about finances and working conditions. A series of increasingly ambitious plans were drafted; to call them unrealistic was heresy or treason. Gosplan was purged of 'pessimists' whose projections for growth were too low and the Party stepped up harassment of 'bourgeois specialists'.

Specialist baiting: The Shakhti Show Trial

'Economic conservatives', who were pessimistic about the Plans, were intimidated into silence. A Communist Party campaign encouraged workers to criticise 'bourgeois specialists' (technicians and managers with a non-proletarian background). This coincided with the dismissal of 'Rightist' academics and the purging from trade unions of supporters of Tomsky by Kaganovich. Neutrality in politics became sabotage. Even children were prosecuted. The highlight was the first major 'show trial'. In a stage-like court room 53 mining engineers from the North Caucasus and Donbas Region were accused of arson, causing accidents, lowering production, importing unnecessary equipment and ruining ventilation. Ten confessed to spying and sabotage on behalf of exiled mine owners and various foreign governments. Although most were acquitted, it was enough to ram home the message that capitalist elements were resisting progress to Socialism and that war would be waged on them. It also warned off any other protesters. An education drive followed, to recruit Communist workers to train as engineers as replacements for those arrested. In this way, the Plans served a political function in mobilising supporters.

---

5 Grain prices were reduced for the 1928 harvest. Instead of money, incentives of better seed, machines or credit were offered, but not enough to satisfy the peasants. Many preferred to pay fines for not delivering enough and then make a profit on the free market. Others sold to poorer neighbours or fattened their animals. Some food grain had to be imported, which infuriated the industrialists.

6 Stalin blamed this crisis on the 'strike of the *kulaks*'. Officials now organised collection on military lines, using emergency powers. Poor peasants were offered a 25 per cent share for making grain confiscations from the rich. However, since most grain was actually grown by middling peasants, the 'class struggle' between rich and poor peasants became a class war against the peasantry in general.

7 At the same time, the State now stepped up the drive against 'Nepmen' to end speculation and control prices and distribution. By the early 1930s, artisans and private shops had gone or joined cooperatives. Peasants were forced into contracts with the State to deliver an annual quota of grain for payment by money or goods. The State repeatedly proved unable to deliver its side of this bargain.

8 Ordered to bring in the quota 'at any price', procurement agents and other officials had no leeway. The targets they were set ignored local harvest situations. Initially, heavy quotas were set for richer peasants, but many of these were quickly impoverished. Next, all 'surpluses' were confiscated which destroyed inter-village commerce, which had traditionally evened out fluctuations in individual farmer's harvests, leaving them vulnerable to famine.

9 Tension in the countryside escalated. To halt 'leakage' of grain, road blocks were used. Carts, barges, barns and huts were searched. Arrests provoked peasant violence against officials who retaliated with armed force. Thousands of volunteer workers, officials, police and troops were sent out to enforce quotas on villages and individual *kulaks*. Local soviets were authorised to impose heavy fines for shortfalls, without going to court. Confiscation, prison or exile became the penalties for 'hoarding' and 'speculating'. Despite these huge efforts in the winter campaign, rises in procurements were insufficient. There was tension in the Party as the 'Rightists' warned against a return to War Communism. However, by the end of the winter they had lost their strongholds in Moscow and the trade unions and were defeated. By the end of 1928 coercion had destroyed the *smychka* but it was only in late 1929 that Stalin revealed his alternative. This shows how policy often lagged behind events.

Was NEP a dead end?

To Trotsky, NEP was deviation from Communism. Other 'Leftists' blamed it for delaying industrialisation and thus being unable to provide goods to exchange for peasant grain, feeling that agriculture, based on small holdings and low levels of expertise, could never develop.

Bukharin had hoped to see rural cooperatives develop, leading to improvements in crops, education and farming methods. With the help of 'implement and horse stations', simple improvements would lead to steady progress. This did happen until NEP stalled in 1927. However, NEP had been left to run itself. Little effort had been put into developing cooperatives, while the few collective farms in existence were in a very poor state. While Soviet researchers had made advances in electrification and diesel engines, little had been invested in agricultural technology. Lenin had estimated that 100,000 tractors would be needed to establish rural Communism. By 1927, the USSR had 28,000 and was only producing 1,000 annually. Plans drawn up in 1924 for a major tractor works at Stalingrad were shelved until 1929.

Bukharin in his 'Notes of an economist' (his surviving statement on the crisis) said that the socialised sector of industry was improving, with investment in industry having doubled. He believed that producing more consumer goods, taxing the *kulaks* to limit their influence and developing cooperatives were the answers. The USSR should resist over-centralisation and keep pace with resources and agriculture. Industry needed to become more efficient and to lower costs.

Historical analysis
Today, experts cannot agree over whether NEP could have worked. True, the economy was back to about 1913 levels but Russia's international position was worsening. Foreign trade had barely climbed to half the 1913 levels and was in deficit. Productivity was slipping behind the West and the technological gap was widening. The USSR's

recovery was achieved with prewar machines. There were social problems too. Although workers' purchasing power exceeded prewar levels after 1925 and the working day came down to 8 hours, unemployment rose to over 1 million. Young workers and women were badly affected. There was also industrial discontent in the trade unions about government orders to prevent strikes and to cooperate with non-Communist specialists. In the towns overcrowding became problem with insufficient houses being built. Moscow alone gained 700,000 new inhabitants during NEP as workers' families settled there. On the streets, crime, drug-trafficking and prostitution were widespread.

Some economists estimate that NEP could never have produced enough capital; while Stephen Cohen believes a restored grain market and industrial development geared to the needs of NEP could have worked. Davies suggests that with a sensible pricing policy, industrial growth rates similar to those before 1914 were possible. Some researchers have used computer simulations to show that without collectivisation and Stalin's plans, the USSR could have done as well. Gorbachev, Soviet Leader in the 1980s, even tried to return to NEP through *Perestroika*. However, in 1927 Stalin and the Party saw crises in crude ideological terms: as sabotage, rather than as economically rational.

While taking tribute from agriculture for industry was probably inevitable, the scale and means were not. Even Molotov agreed that NEP should stay. For him and Stalin, measures against the class enemies (*kulaks*) were more important. Bukharin was also surely right to speak against launching collectivisation without tractors. It is thus puzzling as to why the leadership insisted on such rapid industrialisation and on prematurely forcing peasants into the *kolkhoz*.

1929: collectivisation and the Five Year Plans

For many, the autumn and winter of 1929 is the defining period of Stalin's regime. The onslaught against the peasants and the launching of rapid industrialisation, started a series of events which ended in both the 'Terror' and in victory over the Nazis. Looked at like that, the period appears so coherent that it seems to be part of a deliberate scheme. Examination of 1928–30 tends to undermine this view.

Launching the Five Year Plan

The struggle between rapid industrialisers and economic moderates was resolved in 1928. Stalin's allies, Ordzhonikidze and Kuibyshev, led the charge, promoting policies similar to those of the discredited Preobrazhenski. With Gosplan purged, a series of utopian plans were produced. Kuibyshev's final, 'optimum' version was approved in April 1929 (backdated to October 1928). It anticipated a massive 20% annual growth, surpassing the USA's most rapid decade of industrialisation (1850–60) which had averaged 8.7 per cent annual growth. Priority went to establishing machine tool industries – to reduce reliance on imports, and metals – which were essential to security as well as for machinery and tractors. The targets required other factors to fall into place: good harvests, lower military expenditure, higher quality in industry and increased external trade. These did not occur.

The great leap forward

The Plans were little more than broad targets: e.g. industry was to increase by 180%, consumer goods by 70% and agriculture by 55%. Each enterprise was then told how much of each item had to be produced. These 'quotas' were often wildly optimistic with political pressure to overfulfil them. But by 1930 the Plan was behind schedule, partly due to falling world prices for Russia's raw material exports. Instead of revising it downwards, Stalin and Molotov called for 'The five-year plan in four'. While Kuibyshev – who was closer to the figures – soon realised this was impossible, Stalin continued to proclaim, 'there are no fortresses we Bolsheviks cannot storm'.

The Plan was now the means by which the Communists would transform society. Workers formed 'Socialist emulation brigades', competing to fulfil quotas. OGPU was told that providing exports of timber and minerals took precedence over their other activities. The summer of 1929 saw the establishment of labour camps in the North and East. In 1930 this *gulag* system comprised six camps; by 1931 2 million people were in the *gulags*. The police organised the building of roads and canals, hired out labour and ran their own Siberian 'gold rush'.

Agriculture

Stalin's call for rapid collectivisation in November 1929 came as a surprise. Stalin did not make major speeches on collectivisation until well into the grain crisis, which itself had been unexpected. Even then, little guidance was given to officials on how to collectivise. Without the technology to cope with large farms and huge fields, the move was impractical. Existing collective farms couldn't even accommodate the influx of poor peasants lured by incentives earlier in 1929. Collectivisation resulted from a series of cumulative steps: as with much of the Five Year Plan, policy was allowed to drift.

Coercive measures in 1928 disrupted trade and brought the virtual collapse of handicraft industries. As resistance spread among the disillusioned peasantry, firstly supplies and then the spring sowing were disrupted. In February 1929 bread was being rationed. By April, the regime had its back against the wall, for which Stalin blamed the *kulaks*. The 'Right' protested against Stalin's methods, but he launched a bitter press campaign against them and managed to persuade some – such as Kalinin – to fall into line. Bukharin's allies were convincingly defeated at the Sixteenth Party Congress in April, where Stalin presented his colleagues with a stark choice. Against the backdrop of a massively upgraded Five Year Plan and a widespread belief that they were in a race against time, Stalin asked, '*kulaks* or kolkhozy?'. He drew parallels with Lenin's struggle with the *kulaks* in 1918 and called for that 'old Leninist hardness' in order to make the leap into Socialism.

After successful experiments with collectivisation that summer, Stalin pushed for drastic action in agriculture. Rural communists were ordered to join kolkhozes to set a good example and *Pravda* called for 'all forces' to be used before the 1930 sowing or else industrialisation would fail. The winter of 1929–30 saw three overlapping campaigns:

◢ the procurement campaign
◢ dekulakisation
◢ mass collectivisation.

The grain procurement campaign

The 1929 campaign was the biggest yet. Many urban activists poured into the countryside to help collect grain. It was quite effective and 16 million tons were collected. Unrealistic quotas were set but were enforced irrespective of this. As officials had been punished in 1928 for being too lenient, they did not repeat that mistake in 1929. In the main grain regions, up to one-third of the crop was taken. Officials used new powers to arrest, deport and confiscate the property of those who defaulted on quotas. Those who resisted were labelled 'kulaks'. Stalin told officials to break the kulaks in battle and remove their means of existence.

Dekulakisation

In the campaign against 'kulak speculators', Stalin provided little guidance as to who the kulaks were. According to his class analysis, someone with two horses and four cows was a kulak. 'Ideological kulaks' were any peasants who resisted collection or collectivisation. One could become guilty by association, by appeasing or not opposing kulaks. Stalin's pithy sayings – such as 'when the head is off, one does not mourn for the hair' – encapsulate the lack of sympathy shown. Bands of poor peasants were used to intimidate wealthier or unpopular peasants. Land, tools and animals were confiscated and they were driven out. Peasants tried to avoid labelling by 'self-dekulakisation' (selling or destroying their property). Officials had to cast their net wider. Some went beyond their instructions and sent peasants into exile. The campaign also spread beyond the directed area into poorer areas.

On 27 December 1929 Stalin proclaimed the 'liquidation of the kulaks as a class'. Around 15 per cent of all households were finally dekulakised, well beyond official estimates that 4 per cent of households were kulaks. The campaign also escalated to destroy the peasant way of life. Activists from movements such as the 'Militant Godless League' closed churches, removed their bells (which peasants used to warn of raids) and converted them to stores or stables. Looting was also widespread. Andrle estimates that around 63,000 were imprisoned or killed, around 150,000 exiled to OGPU settlements in the North and East, while a majority were evicted onto marginal land. Probably some 25 per cent migrated voluntarily to avoid punishment. Others were saved by having soldiers or workers among their family members.

◢ Source A

...this unprecedented success in agricultural development is due to the fact that the Soviet government correctly recognised the growing needs of the peasants for modern implements, for modern technique; it correctly recognised that the old forms of cultivation leave the peasantry in a hopeless position, and taking all this into account it came to their aid in good time by organising ... tractor stations and collective farms.

Lastly, this unprecedented success in collective-farm development is due to the fact that the matter was taken in hand by the advanced workers of the country. I am referring to the workers brigades, tens and hundreds of which are scattered in the principal regions of the country ...

What can be surprising in the fact that the workers have succeeded in convincing the peasants of the advantages of large-scale collective farming over individual small farming, the more so as the collective farms and state farms are striking examples of these advantages?

Stalin's speech, November 1919, on 'A year of great change'

1930: mass collectivisation

Once the harvest was in, the next campaign began. From January 1930 an army of 250,000 volunteers and screened conscripts were deployed for crash collectivisation. Urban activist brigades, including the famous '25000ers', *Komsomol* (see key term, page 61) and trade unionists would provide a proletarian elite in the countryside. Supported by police and Red Army troops, they initially used persuasion; but under pressure to achieve results quickly, they used force. They were largely ignorant of the peasants. Some believed the tractors were coming, others were simply doing what they were told. It led to much pressure. At village meetings, activists would lecture and browbeat peasants, announce collectivisation and seize animals for the *kolkhoz*. Local 'class enemies', such as teachers or priests, were lucky to escape with only insults. Liquidation and collectivisation proceeded hand in hand as *kulaks* were barred from entering the new kolkhozes.

Local parties were given targets for numbers of households collectivised, but only vague instructions on how to achieve them. Consequently, officials tried to outdo each other to ensure promotion or went too far rather than risk being seen as 'Rightists'. Stalin encouraged them in his speeches and behind the scenes. Excesses also stemmed from collectivisation competitions promoted by leading Communists such as Bauman, the Moscow Party Secretary. The pace was breakneck, although this was not due to peasant readiness but to Party determination. The centre got the reports it wanted to hear.

Peasant households in kolkhozes	
October 1929	4 per cent
January 1930	21 per cent
March 1930	58 per cent

Rumours about collectivisation added to the chaos: even gold teeth and women were to be collectivised. Hair would be collected for industry or burnt in machines as fuel. Some brigades actually did take household property and cut off peasants' long hair or beards. Serious peasant resistance included murdering officials, arson, rioting and armed risings. Battles were fought in Cossack areas of the Ukraine and serious trouble occurred in the North Caucasus and Kazakhstan. Destroying crops and slaughtering their livestock were the more common protests. Some raided the *kolkhoz* to take their property back. Troops crushed resistance while the Party response to the dangerous fall in livestock numbers was to call for more collectivisation.

Retreat

The Politburo had lost control. It was unprepared for the violence, unrest, speed and scale of the operation. The chaos it had unleashed now threatened the spring sowing, while rebellion posed political dangers. Top officials were sent out to the republics to put down risings. Stalin came under pressure from some colleagues to retreat. In March 1930 he accused officials for misunderstanding his straightforward instructions and being 'dizzy with success'.

◢ Source B

Can it be said that this line of the Party is being carried out without violation or distortion? No, it cannot, unfortunately. We know that in a number of areas in the USSR, where the struggle for the existence of the collective farms is still far from over, attempts are being made to leap straight away into the agricultural commune, 'socialising' dwelling houses, small livestock and poultry; moreover this 'socialisation' is degenerating into bureaucracy decreeing on paper because the conditions which would make such socialisation necessary do not exist. One might think that the grain problem has already been solved in the collective farms, that it is already a past stage, that the principal stage at the present moment is not solution of the grain problem but solution of the problem of livestock and poultry breeding. Who, we may ask, benefits from this blockheaded 'work' of lumping together different forms of the collective-farm movement?

Is it not obvious that such a policy can be to the satisfaction and advantage only of our sworn enemies? How could there have arisen in our midst such blockheaded exercises? . . . They could have arisen only as a result of the blockheaded belief of a section of our Party: 'We can achieve anything!', 'There's nothing we can't do!'

They could have arisen only because some of our Comrades have become dizzy with success and for the moment have lost clearness of mind and sobriety of vision. To correct the line of our work in the sphere of collective-farm development we must put an end to these sentiments.

Stalin's speech, March 1930, entitled 'Dizzy with success'

There was to be a return to voluntary collectivisation and a rehabilitation of some wrongly dekulakised peasants. Many then abandoned the *kolkhoz*. Only 20 per cent of families remained in them by the autumn. The loss of livestock, however, could not be reversed.

Victory over the peasants

The reprieve was temporary. Dekulakisation continued and was 'completed' by May. Once the bumper crop of 1930 was harvested, collectivisation resumed.

Peasant households in collective farms	
1931	50 per cent
1934	70 per cent
1937	90 per cent

Twenty-five million households were soon in 250,000 collective farms providing low-cost food for the State. Unlike the larger-scale *Sovkhoz*, or state farms, most *kolkhoz* comprised around 70 households; quite close to traditional villages in size. In theory, after paying grain taxes, the peasants could divide the 'surplus' among themselves according to labour days worked. Each job, such as milking or ploughing, was given a tariff of 1–6 kilos of grain and each member had to work a minimum number annually. Machine and Tractor Stations (MTS) supplied seed and hired the peasants machinery, for which they paid in grain. MTS had OGPU units attached to ensure compliance. The farm manager

Figure 10 This propaganda poster captures the vision, illusion and military style of collectivisation

would take control of the harvest and ensure taxes in grain or money were paid. Peasants effectively belonged to their *kolkhoz*.

Who were the kulaks?

On average, the richest 3% of peasants owned 2.3 draught animals and 2.5 cows, compared with overall averages of 1.0 and 1.1 respectively: not huge differences. Well under 1% were major hirers of labour or registered as having non-agricultural business. When defined by sown area, *kulaks* included large families farming together. Damage caused by procurements further complicated the picture, as rich became poorer. Without precise definition, *kulak* became a term with scope for interpretation. Worried about inconsistent application, Moscow tried to standardise it in early 1930 by creating three categories and exempting families of Red Army soldiers or industrial workers. It was ignored.

Lynne Viola studied legal journals to examine who was really expelled and persecuted. During major campaigns she found that the better off and resisters were labelled. However, before 1930 and during 1932–4 when there was less outside influence and there was an exodus of young people to the towns, the definition was shaped by traditional prejudices. It wasn't random and it was contrary to Moscow directives. Outsiders – such as 'former people' (ex-Tsarists), rural intelligentsia, seasonal workers, artisans, the economically weak and 'women of ill-repute' – provided the victims. Many of these were needy households which couldn't contribute their share to collective-farm work in a time of shortage (old, infirm, dependants of exiles and soldiers). Many were women. While the victimisation of these targets was rational economically to the peasants, it represented a re-assertion of traditional and patriarchal village values, not Stalin's Socialist ones.

Lenin had warned against using force against the peasants, yet Stalin had done it. Trotsky argued that the USSR could not industrialise by itself; Stalin was doing it. The credibility of the leadership rested on the outcome of these events and the subsequent history of the USSR was shaped by them. The next chapters examine these changes.

Why did Stalin turn left?

Historians are divided over whether we should look for the reasons for the radicalisation of policy to Stalin or to the context of 1927–9.

Intention

Among those who see the answer at the top, Robert Tucker locates the decision in Stalin's imagination in which he played the heroic, Russian Red patriot carrying out his own 'October'. Tucker believes Stalin fabricated the Shakhti show trial to dramatise the war scare and justify his moves. Collectivisation was his deliberate policy and the 'cult of Stalin' was intended to install himself as the philosophical successor to Marx and Lenin. As such he could not be questioned, while his critics became 'counter-revolutionaries'. Like his hero Peter the Great, he would modernise Russia. It is a persuasive argument, but unfortunately Stalin was so secretive that his speeches and written works provide little reliable evidence of why he actually did things.

Many writers credit Stalin with the foresight to prepare the USSR for war even though there was no imminent invasion in 1928. After World War Two he too claimed this as his motive. He may have genuinely believed that the foreign policy crisis represented real danger and that the slow pace of modernisation weakened military strength. Grain shortfalls had also helped undermine the Tsarist regime in 1916. Faced with a choice between smashing opposition or slowing down, Stalin chose the former. Collectivisation would end peasant autonomy by shattering peasant life. Molotov also justified the attack on the *kulaks* by suggesting that it forced the other peasants to 'jump to attention'. Robert Conquest goes further and suggests that the 1932 famine was deliberate policy. Certainly Stalin called for maximum speed and for ruthless methods, yet his instructions were frequently ambivalent. While it could be argued that this was to make the process seem voluntary, Moshe Lewin draws the alternative conclusion that Stalin didn't really know where his policy would lead.

Conceivably, it was an attempt to complete the Bolshevik Revolution – now that the regime was politically secure – by creating *Homo Soveticus* (Soviet Man). Or perhaps it was simply a power manoeuvre by Stalin to outflank his last rival, Bukharin, by cynically stealing the clothes of their defeated opponents on the Left. Since Stalin was a less attractive leader in peacetime than in war, perhaps he required a new struggle.

None of these really explains why particular choices were made. Was such a brutal campaign necessary to make the peasants submit and to meet the increasingly desperate needs of the towns and industry? Was the 'Terror' planned or was it an emergency response? This is a critical issue as many writers see the campaign against the peasants as the foundation of the later purges and of the Stalinist system itself.

Context

Social historians tend to stress that Stalin operated within a situation he did not create. Russian society is both complex and durable. Its impact on events, especially in the long term, was crucial. Stalin was helpless in the face of high labour turnover, sluggish officials and a peasantry who put their care and effort into their own plots rather than the collective farms. Stalin could brutalise them but he couldn't get them to perform how he wanted. 'Stalinism' was but one phase Russian society went through. As Lewin puts it: 'The Party and its ruling strata are not immune to the corrosion by influences and culture that the country, a huge historical laboratory, keeps creating in (keeping) with its traditions.' Therefore we need an understanding of Russian society to comprehend why its collision with Communism was so violent. Recent research makes it clear that Stalin was not acting alone. Many welcomed his new line. The activists in the Moscow organisation were particularly enthusiastic, while many workers and Party members had grown exasperated with what they saw as the corruption of NEP and its failure to meet their aspirations.

In 1928, Stalin and others in the leadership had lost faith with NEP but had no coherent alternative. Conditioned by the Civil War into military-style solutions to emergencies, they responded to the grain crisis with coercion rather than importing grain or consumer goods. Once committed to this, it set off a chain of events which led to increasingly radical outcomes. Initial short-term measures had to be extended. Faced with resistance, the regime needed strongpoints in the countryside. Collective farms offered a way of providing this and enabled easier collection of grain.

1 Write three headings – POLITICS, AGRICULTURE and INDUSTRY – across the top of an A3 sheet. Put in five broad rows, for 1926 through to 1930.

  a Using chapter 1, list the key political events in the first column.

  b As you go through chapter 2, list the key events in the other columns.

  c Next, draw coloured lines to connect linked events. This will identify turning-points. Circle these points.

  d Use the text to identify the relationship between causes and effects and turn lines into arrows.

  e You should now have a web of causation with some division between more or less important causes and decision points.

  f You can use this to help formulate your argument for an essay.

2 Source analysis

Compare sources A and B on pages 49–52 and attempt the questions below. They will test the sorts of skills your course is developing and marks reflect the level of difficulty.

Using source B

  a What does the 'grain problem' mean? (comprehension)   *1 mark*

  b Who are the 'blockheads' and the 'enemies'? (interpretation)   *2 marks*

Using source A

  c In what ways is Stalin's speech an inaccurate description of the real situation in the countryside? (interpretation and understanding)   *5 marks*

Using both sources

  d In what ways does source B contradict Source A? (comprehension)   *6 marks*

  e What reasons can you suggest for this contradiction? (analysis and comparison)   *6 marks*

  f What do the two sources tell us about Stalin's motives and reactions to events during collectivisation? (evaluation, understanding, judgement)   *10 marks*

CHAPTER THREE

'100 YEARS IN 10': THE PLANNED ECONOMY DURING THE 1930S

Objectives

◢ To understand how the Soviet economy of the 1930s functioned

◢ To decide on the results of the Five Year Plans

◢ To establish how successful Stalin was in transforming the USSR.

Contemporary Soviet sources claimed that the Five Year Plans were overfulfilled, although no one accepts this today. Western estimates have varied because it is difficult to decide how one should measure success. There is also the moral dimension of weighing up industrial modernisation against violence and suffering. To understand why results were so uneven we need to grasp what actually went on.

How the plans worked

Gosplan was often so purged it could barely operate and the final 1929 Plan bore little relation to economic reality. It arose from competing versions, none of which had anticipated collectivisation or the skilled labour shortage. All were vague about where resources were to come from. Once targets were set, Party officials coordinated campaigns by workers to demand further increases; targets were frequently doubled. This could happen because the plans were independent of what we think of as economic constraints (costs, profits). Their main function was to mobilise the population to transform the Soviet Union into a new industrial society: a Socialist version of the USA. Once engineers were freed from accountants, they would create the enterprises to achieve it. Communist willpower would overcome obstacles. This optimistic strategy was industrialisation by military-style mobilisation.

◢ Source A

It is sometimes asked whether it is not possible to slow down the tempo a bit… No Comrades, it is not possible!

To slacken the pace would mean to lag behind; and those who lag are beaten. (Russia) was ceaselessly beaten: by the Mongol Khans ... the Turkish Beys ... Anglo-French capitalists ... Japanese barons. She was beaten for her ... military ... cultural ... political ... industrial ... agricultural backwardness. It is the jungle law of capitalism. You are backward, you are weak – hence you can be beaten and enslaved.

We are 50 or 100 years behind the advanced countries. We must make good this distance in ten years. Either we do it, or they crush us.

Stalin's rationale for speed, 1931

A command economy

Since industrialisation was part of Socialism's struggle with its enemies, the economy was run as if at war. The plans were warlike: on the industrial 'front', 'battles' were 'fought' for production by shock 'brigades'. Workers 'battled' conservative experts; peasants 'struggled' with *kulaks*. Their heroism was reported by writers' 'brigades' on the literature 'front' including an American who worked at Magnitogorsk (Source B).

◢ Source B

A quarter of a million souls, communists, kulaks, foreigners, convicts and a mass of blue-eyed Russian peasants building the largest steelworks in Europe in the middle of the Russian steppe. Men froze, hungered and suffered, but the construction went on with a disregard for individuals and a mass heroism unparalleled in history.

*J Scott, **Beyond the Urals** (Secter & Warburg, 1924)*

Like a country at war, the State controlled and allocated all investment and resources. Huge new Party and Government empires were created to oversee economic developments – such as the Commissariat of Heavy Industry, under Grigori Ordzhonikidze. New roles led to new divisions among the 'Stalinists', as those heavily involved with running industry became more realistic and opposed the radicals. In particular, they divided over the pace of change and the methods used to achieve it. Consequently, Party policy zigzagged between favouring conventional management and demanding heroic outbursts. Both 1928–30 and 1934–6 saw over-investment followed by cutbacks. Progress was therefore stormy.

Political goals

Politicians favoured gigantic 'showpiece' schemes which were not always economically appropriate, but in their struggle to overtake the West and recast society had tremendous symbolic significance. Huge projects like the Dnieper dam and the Stalingrad tractor works provided economies of scale but also transformed the landscape; dwarfing the people with pylons and smokestacks. Imported assembly lines, it was hoped, would convert uncultured peasants into workers who really cared about production targets. This 'gigantomania' dominated planning in the early 1930s, although many over-ambitious schemes only started after the Plan had finished. Most politicians knew little about technology. Khrushchev pointed out in 1964, that 'it's easier to contemplate space flights today than it was to contemplate the construction of the Moscow Metro in the 1930s'.

Erratic progress led to the Party becoming involved in arbitrating disputes about targets and resources. Faced with shortages, instead of rationalising or innovating, the Soviet solution was to build and staff another factory. When resources ran out, priority was given to politicians' 'shock projects', others being 'frozen'. So, projects and regions competed for priority, dragging in rival politicians to fight their position: Kaganovich for the Ukraine, Shvernik for the Urals. Sometimes two regions gained identical contracts. Extravagant plans and excessive investment led to squandered resources, strain and crisis. Instead of smoothly following a blueprint, there was flux, improvisation and U-turns. The leadership discovered that once set in motion, industrialisation set off trends they had neither wanted nor anticipated.

Worker enthusiasm

In what was presented as a race against time, there was tremendous idealism among many workers, particularly the young. Enthusiasts flocked to live in tents in Siberia alongside political prisoners while building the great steelworks at Magnitogorsk (see Figure 11). The **Komsomol** encouraged members to form 'shockworkers' brigades' and to show up 'technical conservatives' by demanding higher targets and attempting to smash production norms. Party officials encouraged record breaking. From 1929, Socialist production competitions were held between plants and workers. 'Shockworkers', some of whom even

Figure 11 Young enthusiasts heading for Kuzbass in Siberia

tried to live communally, were given privileges such as extra rations. They often provoked resentment and hostility from older, more conservative workers. Workers who ostracised or attacked them and managers who failed to provide them with supplies of the best equipment were viewed as wreckers, especially if they had bourgeois origins. These divisions created a state of tension in the workplace. However, the benefits of *'storming'* (see overleaf) outweighed other considerations. By 1931 most workers were involved in socialist competitions and by 1935 nearly half were 'shockworkers', including virtually all skilled workers. Eventually, the movement stagnated and many younger workers chose to go into political posts. The Party would later try to resurrect enthusiasm in the Stakhanovite Campaign.

KEY TERMS

Komsomol – young people in the USSR were organised into a variety of political organisations to indoctrinate them and turn them into a future generation of Communist enthusiasts. Children joined the 'Young Pioneers', a sort of Communist Scout movement, while their older brothers and sisters progressed to the Komsomol between 18 and 28. This organisation provided many volunteers for Party programmes and a supplementary force to the police and Red Army. For many, the Komsomol was a stepping-stone to full Party membership.

'Storming' involved working in a superhuman effort to surpass targets, often for over 24 hours at a time. Such efforts were familiar to ex-peasants accustomed to bursts of activity at harvest times and it was ideal for displaying commitment. However, this heroic 'Bolshevik' approach was not ideal for machinery and led to violent fluctuations in output. Many experts favoured a 'scientific approach' to production based on the ideas of Taylor and campaigns to educate the workforce to care about and improve performance by adopting a 'production culture'. Workers should obey experts and through regular effort, master technology and minimalise waste. Policy oscillated between these two extremes.

Problems

1 Skill shortages

Most of the labour force was under 29 and only 20 per cent had five years' experience. 9 million peasants joined the urban labour force between 1929 and 1932. Highly-qualified workers operated beside ex-peasants who had never touched a machine; traditional methods were used alongside American assembly lines. The conveyor belts were sometimes purely symbolic. Thousands of new factories were built without sufficient skilled technicians and engineers, so expensive machines rusted because no one knew how to install or run them. Even where trainees could be sent to the USA and Germany, their new knowledge was not always applicable to the Russian situation with its mixture of primitive and modern methods.

2 Labour turnover

Urban unemployment had disappeared by 1930. Women and migrating peasants found work easy to come by as plants took on extra staff to cope with unpredictable demand. Construction and coalmining, in particular, provided millions of new jobs. It became easy to exchange one job for another, or 'flit' as it became known. R. W. Davies estimates labour turnover in 1929–30 to have been 150 per cent; most workers changed jobs that year, wasting time invested in training them. Ordzhonikidze described the settlements around factories and mines as 'one nomadic gypsy camp'. This 'ruralisation' of industry created additional problems. Peasants used to seasonal working found factory discipline hard to take.

3 'Red tape'

To gain labour, supplies or transport, managers had to obtain permits from administrators. Paperwork, or 'red tape', snowballed, slowing everything down. The sluggishness of bureaucrats (or *Chinovniki*) was due to shortages of secretaries, typewriters and political demands for frequent checks and reports. Efforts by the leadership to speed things up by purging the Chinovniks had little effect.

4 External factors

Food shortages, particularly in 1932–3, reduced rations so far that 'non-priority workers' were at starvation levels. This provoked food riots and a decline in discipline and industrial relations. Also, a security crisis erupted when the Japanese invaded Manchuria. Rearmament and falling grain exports led to a slow-down in imports of machinery. Stoppages became frequent through shortages of materials, lack of spare parts for broken machines or technicians capable of running them. There were strikes, although these were dubbed 'withdrawal of zeal' or 'mass absenteeism'. Communist 'storming' campaigns added to the chaos. By 1932 many projects were incomplete. To the politicians it looked like mismanagement and, in the atmosphere of vigilance fostered by the show trials, it was easy to suspect sabotage.

Managing chaos

Managing industry sounds so bad that it can seem surprising that anyone would do it or even succeed; but they did. Unlike during NEP, the unions were downgraded because of their links with the Right, so enterprises tended to have one-man management. Kaganovich stressed their authority: 'The earth should tremble when the director walks around the plant.' Yet Party officials still kept watch on them. This created tension, as managers resented disruptions to production by Party and *Komsomol* campaigns on issues such as clean changing rooms or learning new skills. These Communist organisations did promote worker discipline through 'comradely courts' but also organised 'criticism campaigns' where managers became the targets.

Sacking or fining workers was little deterrent with so many jobs being created. Workers could appeal and the manager might then be charged with opposing the proletariat. Eventually, in the crisis of late 1932, the regime retreated and reinforced the power of managers. Workers' pay was tied to performance. A day's absence led to instant dismissal, loss of rations, eviction from accommodation and a bar on employment for six months. This was draconian at such a time of hardship.

With constantly moving goalposts and conflicting decrees, managers improvised. Coherent rules did not exist. Managers and workers had to break the rules. Incentives were used to retain specialists and engineers. Managers ignored workers' illegal ways of boosting income. This included machines being set too fast, and lying to or intimidating quality inspectors and Party officials. Many plants cheated by allocating auxiliary workers to help their workers to beat targets. Every year from 1935, Moscow responded by launching a 'norm-tightening campaign'. Boosted wages then fell again, until new scams were developed.

Successful managers were unlikely to be judged on their methods, however unscrupulous. Plants secretly employed extra workers and managers fought to protect their best workers and technicians from various campaigns against 'class enemies'. Even Commissar Ordzhonikidze did this, defending managers against the secret police. To secure resources involved hoarding and constructing unofficial networks to barter. Political patrons were cultivated to secure priorities and protection. Most managers were from political rather than technician backgrounds and since local political officials were also held responsible for production, they had a shared interest. When managers moved, they took their trusted teams with them. To Moscow, these sorts of arrangements smacked of 'localism'. They were wasteful and when such 'nests' were discovered they looked like conspiracies.

The progress of the economy

The great breakthrough years

Between 1928 and 1932 the structure of the Soviet economy was fundamentally altered. The share of gross national product (GNP) from industry, transport and construction rose from 28 to 41 per cent. It 'converted the whole country into a huge building site almost overnight' (Mark Harrison). Yet, there was little overall economic growth. Industrial advances were offset by agricultural collapse.

	1927/8 level	Planned	Achieved 1932
Electricity (billion kWh)	5.0	22	13.5
Agriculture			
(million roubles)	13.1	25.8	16.6
Oil (million tons)	11.7	22	21.4
Steel (million tons)	4	10.4	5.9
Coal (million tons)	35.4	75	64.3
Machinery			
(million roubles)	1,822	4,388	7,362
Consumer goods			
(million roubles)	12.3	25.1	20.2

More problems with grain

Mikoyan, Trade Commissar, took 30 per cent of the record 1930 harvest which paid for imported machinery vital to industrialisation. Similar targets were set in 1931, but that autumn grain supplies dried up. Many agents were sent out to enforce the quotas. Promises to the peasants were broken as grain earmarked for seed, food and fodder was seized by force. Violence erupted in the Ukraine, Caucasus and Kazakhstan with rioting and attacks on procurement officials. These were put down and Stalin called officials who lowered quotas (to enable seed grain to be retained) 'saboteurs'. Exports continued.

Mikoyan was forced to slash his procurement target for 1932 to 18 million tons. The reason was the 'critical food situation' which emerged. By the autumn it was clear that targets were unlikely to be reached, yet Party Secretaries who warned of famine were dismissed as 'deviationists'. As a result, no news leaked out. Stalin refused to respond to appeals in the Party and requisition continued. He also demanded a 'smashing blow' against the collective farmers of the Ukraine who were turning against the government. Peasants everywhere resisted requisition with sabotage, concealing grain and pilfering; so workers were mobilised against 'black-marketeers' and 'resisters'. Tough new laws against theft of grain, with death and exile among the penalties, escalated the zigzag pattern of resistance, reprisals, arrests and deportations. The infamous 'Five stalks law' carried a minimum penalty of five years and 2,110 were sentenced in its first five months. This law gives us an insight into the real nature of the problem: starving peasants

Figure 12 'Landscape Construction': painting by V. V. Rozhdestvenski, 1936. Consider whether this Moscow landscape constitutes 'Socialist realism'.

(nicknamed 'hairdressers') were going out into the *kolkhoz* fields at night and cutting a few ears of grain just to stay alive.

Famine

The winter of 1932–3 saw many rural areas in the grip of a terrible famine. Only in May 1933 did Stalin finally back off, sending a secret circular to Party and OGPU criticising them for indiscriminate arrests and fixing maximum quotas for deportations. Nevertheless, the wave of kulak deportations continued into 1934. Many of the later victims were local officials, who Stalin again blamed for sabotaging his plans. Eventually, Stalin made another policy retreat; grain exports were halted and concessions given to the peasants. In particular, peasants could sell produce from their plots. By 1934 the worst of the famine was over and there were two years of recovery.

A 'Terror' famine?

A number of writers, particularly Robert Conquest, claim the famine was human-made. Its purpose was to eliminate nationalism in the Ukraine and other areas by destroying the will of the peasantry to resist. This version which relies heavily on *emigré* sources, is persuasive; but there are other factors.

◢ Weather: the bumper crop of 1930 encouraged over-confidence, but there were severe droughts in 1931–2.

◢ The decline in livestock: traditional accounts and official sources hold the peasants responsible for eating their animals rather than handing them over to be collectivised, either from resistance or malevolence, depending on who you believe. There were other reasons. Pressure to produce more grain meant abandoning crop rotation and sowing on fallow or grazing land and growing less hay and other fodder crops. Insufficient grain was retained to feed animals over the winters. Recent research by Wheatcroft and Davies suggests this as the key reason for the deterioration in the numbers and quality of livestock.

	1928	1930	1931	1932	1933	1934	1935	1938
Cattle	70.5	52.5	47.9	40.7	38.4	42.4	49.3	50.9
Pigs	26	13.6	14.4	11.6	12.1	17.4	22.6	25.7
Sheep/Goats	146.7	108.8	77.7	52.1	50.2	51.9	61.1	66.6

(Figures in millions. Derived from Nove.)

◢ Traction: while feeding grain directly to people rather than via grain-fed animals was more efficient, it created other problems. In 1928 half of the total means of production in the USSR had been animals. With half of these dead, the country lost a quarter of its capital goods. Less animals meant less draught power to pull ploughs and less manure so the soil became impoverished. With under 200,000 lorries in the entire country, rural transport was devastated by the loss of horses. Collectivisation without mechanisation didn't work. Had tractors been available in 1929 it might have been different.

◢ Misleading data: harvests under NEP had been calculated on the basis of the crop actually gathered and stored. This 'barn yield' was believed to be at best an underestimate, at worst deliberately falsified by *kulaks*. Consequently, statisticians used correcting coefficients. Under political pressure, these were raised until they exaggerated harvests by 20–30 per cent. Modern estimates of the 1932 harvest were 50–55 million tons, which is only 72–79 per cent of official data. Similar overestimates were made with potatoes and sugar beet. By the early 1930s an even more misleading measure was used: the 'biological crop'. This was the maximum possible yield of the standing crop. It was calculated by counting the number of shoots per square metre sample and multiplying it by the total sown area. It ignored the 15 per cent which was typically lost between field and barn, let alone grain which didn't ripen or was lost to weather and pests. As a result, when the State collected 30 per cent of its estimates, it was actually taking over 40 per cent of the actual harvest. Not enough was left to the peasants.

	1928	1930	1931	1932	1933	1934	1935	1938
Grain harvest (max.)	73.3	83.5	69.5	69.6	68.4	67.6	75.0	75.0
Biological crop					89.8	89.4	90.1	
State collection	10.8	22.2	22.8	18.8	23.3	26.3	28.4	29.1
Exports	0.3	4.8	5.1	1.8	1.7	0.8	1.5	2.1
Remainder (max.)	62.5	61.3	46.7	50.8	45.1	41.3	46.6	45.9

(Figures in millions of tons. Derived from Wheatcroft, Lewin and Nove.)

Clearly, State extractions were crucial. Grain continued to be taken for towns and exports despite falling harvests. Whether this was deliberate starvation, incompetence or simply that the leadership believed the peasants were withholding grain and that there was no alternative policy, is not proven. The State was guilty of suppressing news of the famine, thus preventing foreign relief agencies from helping.

Industrial retreat

Chaos, hold-ups and a decline in youthful enthusiasm led to a falling output from mid 1930. Stalin seemed to move towards a more moderate line. In June 1931 his '6 conditions' speech approved measures to help managers retain skilled labour and stabilise production. These included wage differentials, closer attention to costs and an end to 'specialist baiting'. Rabkrin, which had led the wrecker hunts, was purged and later abolished. Trade unions were ordered to concentrate on raising the technical competence of their members. Communist radicals, particularly those in the Komsomol who had organised production communes and collective piece-rates, were denounced as 'petty-bourgeois' or 'leftist blockheads'. There was a reinforcement of hierarchy and proclamations against 'levelling' in the workplace and experiments with workers operating several machines.

Kuibyshev's Second Plan was frequently redrafted during 1932–3. A moderate version was approved, a year late, in 1934. Lower targets than the First Plan were set at 16.5 per cent per annum for industry with emphasis on raising living standards by increasing consumer goods, food processing and housing. It aimed to raise productivity and quality and to assimilate the projects started under the First Plan.

Boom (1934–6)

While 1,500 industrial plants came on stream in the First Five Year

Plan, 4,500 started producing during the Second. The period 1934–6 saw great economic growth. Per capita GNP, productivity and living standards rose after rationing was ended in 1935. By 1937 industry was producing four times the 1928 and 1913 levels. Most of this growth was in heavy industry while consumer goods remained scarce and expensive. With most plants operating piece-rates and higher pay in priority industries, egalitarianism declined. Widening differentials and the distribution of consumer goods according to effort created class division. However, good times for the new elite were shortlived.

Stagnation and crisis (1936–7)

Possibly because of concern that Socialist zeal was declining, or because of changes in the balance of power in the Politburo, there was a political shift to the Left from 1936 with intensified purges and the 'Stakhanovite Movement'. The bulk of Gosplan and many managers were arrested.

Stakhanovites: a political or economic movement?

In August 1935, a coalminer, Alexei Stakhanov, massively overfulfilled his coal quota. As a result, he was made a Socialist hero. By the winter the press was full of reports of smashed quotas and of 'Stakhanovites' struggling against factory enemies. In November, Stalin invited Stakhanovites to the Kremlin and during December, they toured the country exhorting other workers to emulate them. These new proletarian heroes were fêted like pop stars and rewarded with 3–4 times normal wages, access to special shops and priority in housing.

It was a political movement as much as a motivational one. Internationally there had been criticism of Russia's backward labour force. By 1935, most junior workers were ex-peasants and the movement glorified their transformation into proletarian heroes. Within the leadership, it represented a challenge to Ordzhonikidze, who wanted managers to control industry, from those such as Ezhov, who were suspicious of attempts to water down Socialism. Production was disrupted as Stakhanovites demanded the best tools and materials, altered machine settings to speed them up or tried to work several machines at once. When managers resisted this interference, Stakhanovites accused them of being class enemies. Other workers resented their privileges and ostracised or even attacked them.

As with earlier storming campaigns, the Stakhanovite Movement attempted to show that heroic workers could master technology without bourgeois specialists. Economically, it failed, since production increases were usually short term while clever adaptations to machines by some workers were offset by damage to high-quality equipment by others. Politically, it represented a triumph for radicals in the leadership. It also made a contribution to the Terror, as workers were able to denounce their bosses as saboteurs. In early 1936 the movement was criticised for its excesses, perhaps reflecting a victory for Ordzhonikidze, but it recovered following his death. Eventually, some factories had over one-third of their workers labelled as 'Stakhanovite'. As with shockworking, it became a meaningless label and their pay levels fell.

Terrorising managers did not raise production and growth slowed from 1937. Roberta Manning's research suggests that this 'economic crisis' derived from a range of factors:

◢ Shortages of skilled workers
◢ Disruption due to 'Storming' and Stakhanovites
◢ Paralysis as decisions and responsibility were avoided because of fear that honest mistakes would be construed as wrecking.
◢ The purges, which created a shortage of expertise: even key specialists like the aircraft designer Tupolev had to work from jail. However, some researchers (*e.g.* Manning) see the purges as resulting from the economic slowdown, rather than the other way round.
◢ Rearmament to meet the threat from Germany and Japan (*e.g.* tractor output fell to half of 1936 totals because production lines were switched to making tanks). As military investment quadrupled, other factories were unable to buy raw materials and replacement parts. This increased breakdowns and stoppages.
◢ Continued bottlenecks in fuel, transport and construction materials which held up the rest of industry.

◢ The poor harvest of 1936 which severely reduced food supplies.

◢ The hard winter of 1937 crippled fuel supplies, bringing transport and industry to a standstill.

◢ A slump in world trade, especially in heavy goods.

Reaction and the Third Plan (1938)

Initially there was a search for scapegoats and the management of Stalingrad Tractors and other showpiece concerns were attacked in the press for wasting funds. However, as in 1933, there was pressure within the Politburo to rein in the police and to adopt a more conservative policy. NKVD boss Ezhov was replaced in 1938 and new measures strengthened the power of managers. Harsh labour laws required workers to carry workbooks recording their performance and gave them the sack if they were 20 minutes late. Three lates counted as an absence which resulted in imprisonment or compulsory labour. Permission was required to change jobs. To ensure obedience, managers were prosecuted for not enforcing these laws, doctors were punished for signing people off sick unnecessarily and judges for being too lenient.

Reality was more complex. Despite the risks, most managers colluded with workers to evade these rules. Whether from sympathy or to keep good workers, regulations were broken. In any case, few managers were able to provide workers with the required safety equipment or even their wages on time. Valuable workers were retained with secret wage supplements or by giving workers higher skill gradings which would raise their pay. Some managers fed their workers as well.

Meanwhile, Nikolai Voznesenski, a brilliant economist, was appointed to rebuild Gosplan in 1938. His 1939 Plan gave priority to defence and heavy industry but included no gigantic schemes. Ironically, there was also a drive to master techniques and defer to the expertise of engineers and technicians. This was exactly what those who suffered in the purges had wanted. In the years up to the Second World War, growth continued to slow as the armed forces were expanded from 1.5 million to 5 million and emphasis was given to completing unfinished projects, rather than starting new ones.

Measuring the success of the Five Year Plans

◢ Source C

We have not only created these new great industries but have created them on a scale and dimensions that eclipse the scale and dimensions of European industry.

And, as a result of all this, the capitalist elements have been completely and irrevocably ousted from industry, and socialist industry has become the sole form of industry in the USSR.

And, as a result of all this, we have succeeded by the end of the fourth year of the five year plan period in fulfilling the total programme of industrial output, which was drawn up for five years to the extent of 93.7 per cent.

It is true that we are six per cent short of fulfilling the total programme of the five year plan. But that is due to the fact that in the view of the refusal of neighbouring countries to sign pacts of non-aggression with us, and the obligations that arose in the Far East, we were obliged for the purpose of strengthening our defence, hastily to switch a number of factories to the production of modern defensive means. And, owing to the necessity of going through a certain period of preparation, this switch resulted in these factories suspending production for four months, which could not but affect the fulfilment of the total programme of output for 1932, as fixed in the five year plan.

It is beyond any doubt that, but for this incidental circumstance, we would almost certainly not only have fulfilled, but even over-fulfilled the total production figures of the five year plan.

Finally, as a result of all this, the Soviet Union has been converted from a weak country, unprepared for defence into a country mighty in defence, a country prepared for every contingency, a country capable of producing on a mass scale all modern means of defence, and of equipping its army with them in the event of an attack from abroad.

Stalin's verdict on the First Five Year Plan, January 1933

It is difficult to use conventional measures to assess the USSR because of the nature of the economy. For example, while industrial capital doubled, another major item, livestock, halved. Many figures are uncertain because of different methods of calculation.

1 Gershenkron effect

Growth depends on the point of comparison. Soviet statistics used 1926 prices as their index with which to compare progress. In 1926 machinery was rare and expensive so since machines were a major growth area this inflates their value. Western economists working back from 1937 values do the opposite (Figure 13).

Price of tractors		Output of tractors	
1926	50	1926	10
		1930	15
		1932	20
1937	30	1937	30

Using the Soviet model, the value of tractor production doubled between 1926 and 1932 (10x50 to 20x50). Using the Weston model, the value of tractor production only rose by 20% (10x50 to 20x30).

Figure 13 Model of Gershenkron effect

2 Hidden inflation

Soviet statistics fix the prices of new goods when they first appeared, not at 1926 prices. Since most commodities rose in price over time, this also inflates values.

3 Political considerations

It was not just the USSR which required propaganda. During the Cold War there was a tendency to overrate the Soviet economy because it had beaten the Germans and because the western military had to justify their levels of defence spending to combat the 'Red Menace'. Some major economic research was sponsored by the United States Air Force!

Soviet figures for annual growth were around 17 per cent from 1928 to 1940. Western estimates range from 7 to 13.6 per cent per annum. Even the lowest is a considerable achievement. Structural change was even more impressive. The Plans created a large, diverse industrial base, spreading industry beyond its original centres to Central Asia (textiles) and Siberia (coal and metals). Entire new industries, such as vehicle and aircraft manufacture, were established. By the late 1930s, the USSR was building all equipment, from concrete mixers to turbines, rather than importing them. Russia became a leading producer of power (electricity, coal and oil), while top-quality steel was manufactured at modern works such as Zaparozhe on the Dniepr, next to the largest hydroelectric scheme in Europe. New cities were built, including Magnitogorsk in the Urals. Cheliabinsk was massively expanded with a tractor works, while Novosibirsk became the 'Chicago of Siberia'. Huge infrastructure projects included canals, the Moscow metro and the redesigning of the new capital. Between 1928 and 1937, per capita GNP in the USSR increased by 60 per cent, a figure which easily surpassed other nations. It did this at a time of world economic depression.

These achievements mask huge contradictions. Quantities were impressive but quality and productivity remained low. Bread production was industrialised, smiths became mechanics and the economy was dominated by huge plants in the machine building and metals sectors – yet agriculture remained a disaster and quotas of consumer goods were unfulfilled. Over-investment created further problems for the economic system over the long term. There was also waste.

Khrushchev provides a good example of the results of emphasising quantity over quality. His investigation of bursting Russian tyres found that 'one or two layers of cording had been eliminated...(and) the amount of reinforcing wires had been diminished to make the process more economical'. As a result, tyres lasted a tenth of the time of American models. The factory surpassed its quotas, but with useless tyres. The mixed picture of success and failure can be illustrated by examining different areas of the economy.

Key sectors of the economy

Agriculture

Aside from the devastating famine of 1932–3, agriculture consistently failed to meet its targets (see Figure 14 overleaf). Rises in output were offset by population rises. This problem persisted to the end of the Soviet Union. There were some successes but not enough:

◢ Industrial crops: cotton harvests, boosted by investment in Central Asia, tripled in the decade after 1928 and despite rising demand replaced imports. However, when grain distribution broke down, the farmers who had been ordered to grow it found that cotton was no substitute for food. The *kazakhs*, in particular, suffered famine as a result. Of the other textiles, flax failed to keep up, while wool and leather output never recovered from the loss of livestock.

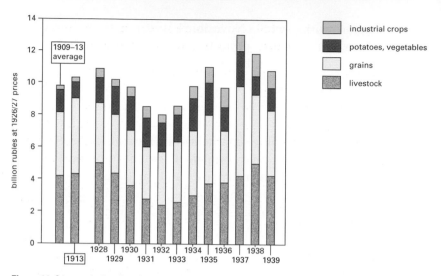

Figure 14 Gross agricultural production 1909–13 to 1939 (Source: Wheatcroft and Davies)

◢ Mechanisation: many thousands of tractors and combines were produced which enabled 95 per cent threshing, 72 per cent ploughing, 57 per cent spring sowing and 48 per cent of grain harvests to be mechanised by 1938. However, cultivation of beet, hay and sunflowers remained unmechanised. For most of the 1930s supplies of agricultural machinery was inadequate. It was only at the end that combined horse and tractor power exceeded that of 1928. Unlike American, intensive labour was extensively used alongside machines, to weed, bind and reap grain.

◢ Expertise: the initial purges of 'disloyal' agronomists (agricultural economists) undid much of the progress made under NEP. Most Party Secretaries lacked farming experience so many mistakes were made. Few people had experience of large-scale fields, let alone tractors; most peasants had never seen one. Much expertise was lost in the dekulakisation campaign and there was considerable political interference with farm management. The ideal size of collective farms, for example, was changed several times. There was an extensive programme to train tractor and combine drivers and a three-fold increase in specialists (vets, agronomists, *etc.*). However, few of these actually worked on farms; most were in research and development, or training.

⬛ Research lead to improved seed bank and work on artificial insemination raised stock quality, but its impact was limited.

⬛ Weather: there was some improvement in the organisation of collections and distribution, which prevented a famine after the poor 1936 harvest. However, the main reason famine was absent until 1946 was because of an unusually drought-free spell. When drought returned in 1946, it led to another famine. Luck therefore played a significant role before and during the Second World War.

⬛ Peasants: the problem remained the unwillingness of the peasants to deliver what the State wanted. The success of their plots testified to their potential; by 1936, these comprised under 5 per cent of farmland but contributed a quarter of total production. Most of the USSR's vegetables and a massive 67 per cent of meat and dairy produce came from these plots, but little grain. Peasants relied on the *kolkhoz* for grain and their plots for food. The Party kept clamping back on this peasant economy as it was clear where energies were going, yet the concession remained. Paradoxically, while collectivisation destroyed the life pattern and economic system of the peasantry, it reinforced traditional outlooks. As the young and educated left for the industrial towns, the villages became more conservative. The majority retained their religious beliefs. The numbers of adults farming fell from 61 to 48 million between 1926 and 1939. Output per adult did rise but this was largely due to the enormous number of extra hours they had to work. Productivity remained low. Production didn't officially recover to 1920s levels until 1960.

Millar's recent study suggests collectivisation didn't work solely to the disadvantage of agriculture. Farmers were increasingly able to buy consumer goods while agricultural machinery represented a capital transfer to the countryside. However, most writers conclude that peasants paid a high price for industrialisation.

Technology

A choice had to be made between the German model of technology, where skilled workers used general-purpose machines, and the American one where expensive specialised machines mass-produced standard designs using semi-skilled workers. Neither was appropriate for a developing country like Russia, which had plenty of labour, but little skill and capital to treat machines as disposable, like America did. In the event the US model was preferred. Russian industry changed course and became 'Americanised'. Entire plants were copied. Magnitogorsk was based on the US steel plant at Gary, Indiana, while the auto works at Nizhni Novgorod was modelled on a Ford factory.

Although remaining behind the USA, the USSR caught up with Europe in many areas by 1940. Many of the Soviet machines were newer than European ones, although they were not always updated. Despite the ruin of research by the purges, there was still innovation. Soviet designers developed motorcycles and cameras, while chemists made advances in plastics and pioneered synthetic rubber production.

However, technological advances were not critical to performance and new machines were concentrated in a few sectors. If possible, machines were replaced with cheap labour. The construction industry continued to rely on bricks and timber not concrete. Not all the technology was appropriate. US technology was designed to meet American problems; the Soviet situation was different. They needed to turn out a limited range of products in huge quantities, using their large supply of low-skilled labour. They didn't need machines as sophisticated and expensive as the American models. Enthusiasm for foreign technology neglected Russia's own strengths and specialisms.

Transport

Transport was starved of investment in the Plans and despite heroic efforts with basic equipment contributed greatly to industrial bottlenecks.

Railways were expected to carry massively increased loads to and from remote, new industrial projects. Major shortages of wagons, fuel (especially during the coal famine of 1937/8) and storage space resulted. By late 1930, 2 million precious tons of grain were stranded at stations, and in 1931 some industries had to shut down due to lack of supplies. Political interference, particularly by Kaganovich, was unhelpful. He scrapped a Soviet diesel project just as it neared success and imported huge, and thus impressive, American locomotives. These proved too heavy for Russian rails to bear. 'Storming' with trains wasted fuel, wore out equipment and was highly dangerous. By 1939 the railways were incapable of supplying the Army adequately in the war against Finland.

New canals added to the water transport network, but were underused. Outdated equipment and long freeze-ups made them unreliable. Despite building barges on the Volga, water transport remained inefficient.

Roads remained poor and impassable in bad weather. It was not until 1943, when military engineers built roads for the advancing Red Army, that things improved. Similarly, there were relatively few lorries until the influx of Allied aid from 1942 onwards. In this respect, Russia came out of the War with better road transport than when they entered it.

Arms

Defence was important from the outset (see Figure 15). In 1932 arms outstripped tractor production. By 1938 over half of iron and steel, and much high-grade fuel and metals, went to make arms. It demanded high technology, was top priority and offered the best pay.

Tanks were built from scratch. The first in 1930–31 were copies of British and American models. By 1939 production was underway on Soviet designs, such as the T34 and KV Heavy models. The Katyusha system pioneered rocket design and the latest military aircraft, such as the Yak, matched those in the West. Despite this, much Russian weaponry was obsolete. Most aircraft production was small scale, based on foreign models and required imported engines.

Attempts had been made to locate industry east of the Urals and away from invasion. However, during the Third Five Year Plan much was built in European Russia, because costs were lower and also because of Stalin's confidence that invasion was impossible. Plans were laid to convert tractors into tanks, but this did not prove easy.

Commerce

Soviet Russia had a love–hate relationship with the West. Despite hostile rhetoric the USSR recognised its deficiencies in technology and technologists. There were originally some joint ventures although, after their experience of the revolution, most capitalists were reluctant to invest and had pulled out by 1930, interested in obtaining raw

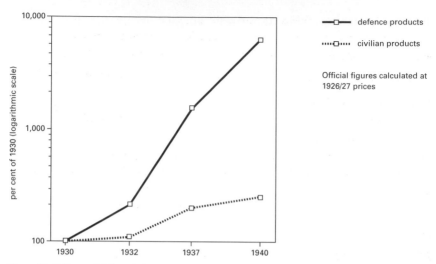

Figure 15 Civilian and defence industry, gross output 1930–40. These are official figures, calculated at 1926/7 prices. (Source: R. W. Davies)

materials rather than developing Russia. During the First Five Year Plan, German and US contractors were hired to provide expert assistance.

Trade took until 1931 to regain prewar levels. Imports were controlled to prevent a deficit and were restricted to the means of production, not consumption. By the mid-1930s, there was a surplus and debts were repaid but trade stagnated after that, due to the world depression.

Within the USSR, a private sector persisted. As late as 1935, 25 per cent of artisans and over 2 million small-scale manufacturers remained outside the cooperative system. Market forces survived in the barter networks of managers, the selling of produce from peasant's plots and the movement of workers between jobs for better wages or conditions. The free market was renamed the 'collective farm market' in 1936 so that Socialism could be officially declared.

Conclusion

Overall, rapid structural change was accomplished with spectacular growth in industry, urbanisation and GNP but the USSR remained unproductive and poor. It did not win the economic race with the West, which makes its victory against Nazi Germany remarkable.

TASKS

1 Essay to evaluate similarity and difference
This popular format requires you to identify criteria and then to find
evidence for and against a particular viewpoint in order to evaluate it.

'How successful was Stalin's economic programme during the 1930s?'

This breaks down into:
- Assuming he had a programme, what were his aims? (Political and social as well as economic)
- What would constitute success for each of these aims?
- What evidence is there of a) success and b) failure from the period?
- Where does the balance lie (*e.g.* 'largely successful')
- How does your verdict compare with those of historians?

Using lists may help clarify your ideas:

AIM   CRITERIA FOR SUCCESS   FOR   AGAINST

2 Analytical skills
The ability to interrogate material critically is one of the most prized skills
learned by history students. You can develop it by practising asking key
questions of a source (*e.g.* Source D).

Source D

Without expecting to convince the prejudiced, we give, for what it may be
deemed worth, the conclusion to which our visits in 1932 and 1934 and subsequent
examination of the available evidence now lead us. That in each of the years
1931 and 1932 there was a partial failure of crops in various parts of the huge
area of the USSR is undoubtedly true. It is true, also, of British India and of the
United States. It has been true, also, of the USSR and of every other country
of comparable size, in each successive year of the present century. In countries
of such vast extent, having every kind of climate, there is always a partial failure
of crops somewhere. How extensive and how serious was this partial failure of
crops in the USSR, in 1931 and 1932, it is impossible to ascertain with any
assurance. On the one hand it has been asserted by people who have seldom
had any opportunity of going to the suffering districts, that throughout huge
provinces there ensued a total absence of foodstuffs, so that ▓▓▓▓▓▓▓▓▓▓
literally, several millions of people died of starvation. On the other hand, Soviet
officials on the spot, in one district after another, informed the present writers
that, whilst there was a shortage and a hunger, there was at no time a total lack
of bread, though its quality was impaired by using other ingredients than wheaten
flour; and that any increase in the death-rate due to disease accompanying
defective nutrition occurred in only a relatively small number of villages. What
may carry more weight than this official testimony was that of various resident
British and American journalists who travelled during 1933 and 1934 through
the districts reputed to be the worst affected and who declared to the ▓(US)
▓▓▓▓▓▓▓ that they had found no reason to suppose that the trouble had been

81

more serious than was officially represented. Our own impression, after considering all the available evidence, is that the <u>partial failure of crops certainly extended to only a fraction of the USSR: possibly to no more than one-tenth of the geographical area.</u> We think it plain that this partial failure was not in itself sufficiently serious to cause actual starvation, except possibly in the worst districts, relatively small in extent. ⎫ ⑤

This is not to deny that there were whole districts in which drought or cold seriously reduced the yield. But there are clearly other cases, how many we cannot pretend to estimate, in which the harvest failures were caused not by something in the sky but by something in the collective farm itself. ⎫ ⑨ ⓗ

 As we have already mentioned, we find a leading personage in the ~~~~ Ukrainian revolt ~~~~ claiming that 'the opposition of the Ukrainian people', caused the failure of the grain-storing plan of 1931 and still more so that of 1932. He boasts of the success of the 'passive resistance which aimed at a systematic frustration of the Bolshevik plan for the sewing and gathering of the harvest'. He tells us plainly that owing to the efforts of himself and his friends, whole tracts were left unsewn, and, ~~~~ when the crop was being gathered last year (1932), ~~~~ in many areas especially in the south, 20, 40, and even 50 per cent was left in the fields and was either not collected at all or was ruined in the threshing. ⎫ ⓗ

So far as the Ukraine was concerned, it is clearly not Heaven which is principally to blame for the failure of the crops but the misguided members of many of the collective farms. → ⓑ

ⓐ ◄——— Webb, Sidney and Beatrice (*1935*) *Soviet Communism, A New Civilisation,* (London: Longman, Green and Co.) pp. 200–1 ——► ⓒ

Figure 16 'The famine'

a Provenance: Who were the Webbs and are their views significant?

b Context: How might this date affect the availability of evidence and the questions being asked?

c Audience and purpose: What is implied by the title and first line.

d Reliability: The Webbs were 'eye witnesses', as were the sources they cite. Does this mean we should accept them as reliable? (Try to imagine how they gathered the evidence.)

e Style: How do they undermine those who spoke of famine?

f Selection/presentation: Does one-tenth sound bad?

g Plausibility: What mitigation do they offer for crop failure? Is it valid?

h Selection: Is their explanation of the causes of failure sufficient?

i Language and tone: Have these been used throughout to create an impression?

j Validity: How does their account compare with the evidence in this chapter? How do you explain any discrepancies?

3 Try a similar exercise with Stalin's speech (source C on page 73).

CHAPTER FOUR

PARANOIA OR PLOT: WHY DID THE PURGES HAPPEN?

Objectives

⊿ To establish what the Purges were
⊿ To explain why the Purges took place
⊿ To study various historians' explanations of the Purges.

Context

Recent archaeological discoveries of mass graves from Stalin's time, such as those in the Kuropaty Forest outside Minsk, have reopened debates about how many people died in the 1930s and why. As with Hitler and the Holocaust, we want a rational explanation of the reasons for this extraordinary bloodletting in which at least a million died. The issue of what the **Purges** were and why they happened is central to the broader debate about the nature of Stalin's regime.

> ## KEY TERM
>
> **Purges** – in the USSR, *Chistka* refers to the practice of checking on the calibre and documentation of Party members and 'cleaning out' those who were not up to scratch. This was peaceful and those expelled were often readmitted. It reflects an old debate in the Party about whether only committed and active members were acceptable. *Chistkas* occurred in 1921 and 1929, as well as 1933. The intense period of killing from 1937–8 was different, and was known as the *Ezhovchina* in Russia after the NKVD boss. The Western totalitarian view lumps all these events together with the show trials as 'The Purges'. Revisionists (see key term, page 85) see them as different and sometimes contradictory phenomena.

The traditional view is that as Stalin was dictator he must have directed the Purges and known about their scale. If so, then the answer to the question 'why?' lies in his motives and state of mental health, particularly after the suicide of his second wife in 1932. A related view holds the Soviet system responsible, with the killings as the inevitable consequence of Communism and Lenin as much to blame as Stalin since he set up the one-party state. Understanding lies in tracing the progressive build-up of the coercive machinery of the State (Party, police and propaganda) from the 1920s until it could be unleashed in the linked phenomena labelled 'The Purges'.

These views are often referred to as the **totalitarian thesis** (see Figure 17). They provide a model of a disciplined police state, commanded from the top, which used terror systematically to destroy opponents and to cow the population.

However, much recent research has shifted the focus away from Stalin to the wider structures of Soviet society. Stalin delegated internal security to Yenrikh Yagoda and Narkom Ezhov. Did the NKVD (Interior Ministry) take the initiative? Also, did they – as Stalin later claimed – go too far? At a lower level were many Soviet citizens who denounced their neighbours, workmates and even families. Did the purge take on a momentum of its own and infect society like a witch craze? Should

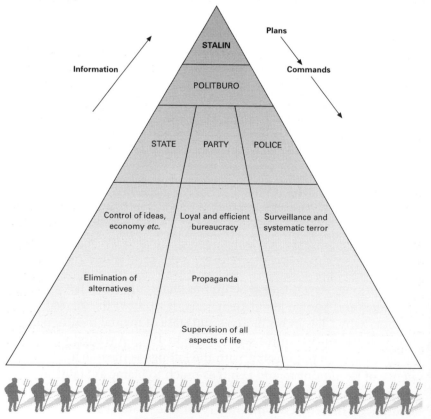

Figure 17 The Totalitarian Model

we even talk of 'the purges'? Perhaps there were a variety of reasons and agencies involved in widely differing events. For example, some killings may have been the result of attempts by collectivising agencies to force economic change through, while others may have been instigated by the NKVD for political reasons. Rather than a united leadership, pursuing clear goals via a monolithic state, perhaps a divided leadership argued among themselves. In reacting to events beyond their control, they produced confusing policy zigzags which enabled lower officials to block or manipulate instructions. Some writers express surprise that government functioned at all.

Ideas which challenge the view that the leadership was directly responsible or planned the purges are usually referred to as ***Revisionist.***

Key Term

Revisionist is the term used when one set of ideas have dominated historical accounts for a long period, but then new ideas emerge to challenge. A well-known example are the works of Hans Mommsen and Martin Broszat on Nazi Germany, which undermine the belief than Hitler was a 'strong dictator' who controlled decision-making in the Third Reich. Soviet Revisionist ideas challenge the orthodoxy that Stalin's policies were necessary. Western Revisionism undermines the image of the USSR as an efficient dictatorship, completely controlled by Stalin. They replace this view with one bordering on chaos (see Figure 18).

Schools of history

A variety of labels are applied to works on Stalin's Russia. Those which explain events in terms of Stalin himself are dubbed 'Stalincentric' or 'Intentionalist' and share the underlying assumption that history is made by 'great men/women'. They vary over whether they see Stalin as god-like (hagiography), excessive but a force for progress (apologists) or evil and destructive (demonology). Soviet Revisionists in the 1980s moved from the first two positions towards the third. Structuralists explain the causes through a far wider range of factors, in particular economic and social forces. Western Revisionism is structuralist, drawing on studies of particular organisations, phenomena and localities. These labels can lead to over-simplification of a writer's position and should be treated with caution (see chapter 6).

As you read on, decide whether you agree with the Totalitarian model or the ideas of the Revisionists. It might help if you try task 1 on page 101.

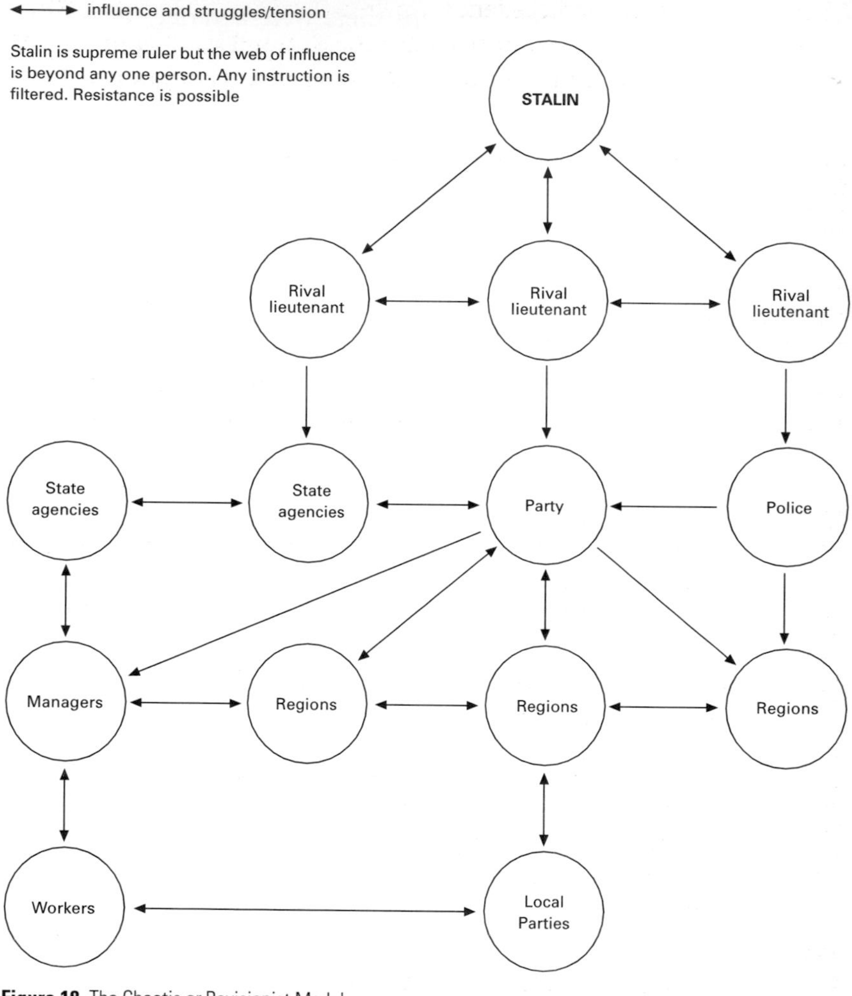

◄──────► influence and struggles/tension

Stalin is supreme ruler but the web of influence
is beyond any one person. Any instruction is
filtered. Resistance is possible

Figure 18 The Chaotic or Revisionist Model

The development of coercion under Stalin

Lenin started the Cheka under Dzerzlinski to use terror to destroy opponents. In 1921 Lenin had outlawed opposition within the Party, expelling thousands who would not accept his 'general line'. Arbitrary arrest and execution had become common during collectivisation.

There was, therefore, a precedent for purging the Party. However, while Stalin inherited OGPU – an instrument for eliminating enemies of the State – terror had not yet been used against Communist Party members.

Operation	% expelled
1921 *Chistka*	25
1929 *Chistka*	11
1933 *Chistka*	18.5
1935 Verification of Party documents	9

Most of those purged from the Party were for personal defects rather than for ideological reasons. Looked at chronologically, there seems to be a number of phases of centralisation and coercion.

1928–30 Show trials of 'Wreckers' and the 'Industrial Party'
Expulsion of over 100,000 'passive', 'ill-disciplined' and 'alien' Party members
Elimination of the *kulaks*
Defeat of Bukharin and purge of Rightists from unions and government
Centralised planning by Gosplan

1930–3 Growth of Gulag system to over 2 million prisoners
Trials of defeated old Bolsheviks
Harsh Labour Laws imposed on workers
Famine – some call it a terror famine against the peasants
Suicide of Stalin's wife as a protest?
Trial of Riutin; expulsion of thousands of 'Riutinites'
Metro-Vickers trial of saboteurs
Party *Chistka*

1934 Assassination of Kirov
OGPU merged in NKVD under Yagoda

1935–6 Verification and exchange of Party Documents

1936–7 Arrest and Trial of 'Leftists' and Trotskyists
Execution of old Bolsheviks (Kamenev and Zinoviev)
Army Purge
Ezhovchina – the time of Ezhov

1938 Trial and execution of Bukharin and Rykov
Execution of foreign Communists

1939 Beria replaces Ezhov and purges the NKVD.

Progressive or parallel developments?

The above list could suggest a systematic build-up both in terms of numbers and status of victims. Similarly, there are a number of components which seem to feature in many of the events of the 1930s, such as the discovery of opposition plots, amazing confessions, networks of conspirators, show trials, and punishment in the 'Gulag' system. Many of these features can be recognised from the 'specialist baiting' of the First Five Year Plan but none of this proves that it was one process.

Was there an opposition?

Soviet historians saw the Purges as a response to threats to the security of the USSR. Some Western writers have seen them as moves by Stalin to crush discontent and opposition which threatened his position.

Industrial enemies

In the 1928 'Shakhti Trial', Vyshinski prosecuted specialists who confessed to being spies and saboteurs and denounced each other. Many of them had been broken by continuous interrogation. In 1930, food scientists and bacteriologists were shot after confessing to wrecking and half the engineers in the Donbas region were arrested for 'bourgeois leanings'. In 1931, Ordzhonikidze, who needed these workers to keep industry going, persuaded Stalin to stop. Despite this, there was a further trial of Metro-Vickers engineers in 1933. Stalin referred to these opponents as Mensheviks or the 'Industrial Party'. Were they?

Machines broke down and targets were not met. This is not surprising considering the numbers of unskilled workers involved and the long hours worked. But this was not sabotage. Some of those accused were foreigners, while others were Russians who worked with them. It is possible that some were spies. This does not explain the execution of many specialists and imprisonment of thousands of others.

Here are a some other possibilities:

◢ Stalin 'deliberately fabricated' evidence to 'dramatise the war danger'. (Robert Tucker)

◢ Terror among the technical intelligentsia was created to whip up production.

◢ The 'militant millenarian atmosphere' (Edward Acton) of the period meant that any criticism was perceived as treason.

◢ Communist workers resented the privileges given to bourgeois specialists. Since Stalin told them that they were fighting a class war against the bourgeoisie they were prone to interpret mistakes made by former class enemies as deliberate.

In rural areas there was resistance to collectivisation which fused with 'bourgeois-nationalist' discontent in some republics, notably Kazakhstan and the Ukraine. If there ever was a 'peasants' party' it was ineffectual. The risings and murder of officials in opposition to the destruction of churches and dekulakisation were uncoordinated and localised. These events were not instigated or exploited by senior political figures or foreign powers.

Political enemies

From Paris, Trotsky remained a leader in exile. There is evidence to support his claims of a network in Russia although it seems likely that this was largely for communication and that it was infiltrated by the NKVD. Many of his old supporters (Radek, Piatakov *etc.*) returned to Stalin after his 'left turn' and were entrusted with key posts. Many old 'Rightist' and 'Leftist' leaders had been similarly rehabilitated. In any case to the mass of Party members who had joined since 1929 Kamenev, Zinoviev and even Bukharin were 'has beens'. None of them were close to the centre of power and while they may have corresponded, there is no evidence that they plotted against the leadership. There were Western agents in the USSR, but there is no proof of their links to senior politicians.

Internal enemies

If the government was run by 'Stalinists' who agreed on the 'general line' and presided over and controlled institutions already cleansed of old opponents, where could treasonous activity occur?

Due to the closed and secret nature of debate in the USSR it is difficult to reach firm conclusions about the degree of divisions among the Stalinist leadership of the early 1930s. There was criticism of the degree of bureaucracy, industrial turmoil and rural disaster in 1930 by Sergei Syrtsov, the Russian President, and by Beso Lominadze, the Transcaucasian Party boss. Should we interpret this as debate or opposition?

If the latter, was it against Stalin or an appeal to him against Molotov or Kaganovich? It started a pattern, whereby 'realists' who had to make things work quarrelled with those concerned with Party discipline. Realists objected when the police arrested valuable specialists who may have once been Mensheviks, or had visited Germany. Most differences were not about goals but the pace and methods of attaining them. The dithering over the targets for the Second Five Year Plan testifies to debate between radicals led by Molotov, who believed that Bolshevik enthusiasm was enough, and realists who wanted to improve the quality of production. As a result, the general line did fluctuate. Should we see this as evidence of opposition to Stalin or of lively politics in the leadership with Stalin standing back to let his lieutenants fight it out and then selecting from different options?

Increasingly, central government faced the problem of local officials not carrying out Moscow's instructions. Regional bosses resisted what appeared as unattainable targets and formed networks ('nests' or 'families') of contacts to secure resources and protection. Initially, the leadership identified this as being due to indiscipline and the low quality of recruits, rather than treason. In trying to regain control of the Party, disputes developed between Kirov and Zhdanov who wanted to use education and propaganda to improve the Party, and Ezhov and Malenkov who preferred to use purges. Numbers expelled even in 1935–6 were not exceptional and were largely for drunkenness or desertion, not opposition.

The Riutin Affair, 1932

Riutin, one of the Moscow leadership, launched a direct attack on Stalin in his widely-circulated 'platform'. He called Stalin an 'evil genius' and called for his removal because of the damage his policies had done. Stalin wanted Riutin dead but while many 'Riutinites' were expelled (*e.g.* anyone who had seen the document), the Politburo refused to execute Riutin. It may be that the other leaders were asserting Lenin's principle of collective leadership against an increasingly autocratic Stalin. Alternatively, they may not have seen Riutin as a threat, or didn't want to establish the principle of shooting Bolsheviks. Some historians see this affair as evidence of opposition. They cite the moderation of policies from 1933, when many opponents of collectivisation were released and NKVD powers restricted, as proof.

'Intentionalist' accounts see this as the point where a vengeful Stalin decided he needed an excuse to eliminate these opponents; after all, Riutin and almost half the 1933 Politburo were dead within five years.

Kirov	assassinated, 1934
Ordzhonikidze	heart attack' (almost certainly suicide) 1937
Kuibyshev	'heart attack', 1935
Kossior	executed, 1939

Stalin, Voroshilov, Kalinin, Molotov and Kaganovich survived.

The Kirov murder, 1934

Sergei Kirov, the popular Leningrad Party leader, was seen by many as a potential successor to Stalin. Historians who believe that Stalin orchestrated the Purges believe that he arranged Kirov's assassination; or, if not, he capitalised on it.

The case for Stalin's involvement relies on motive and connections

◢ Kirov was a liberal, who had resisted Stalin over the economy and repression.

◢ At the 'Congress of Victors' in 1934 Kirov received more support than Stalin, although the ballots were secretly destroyed to conceal this.

◢ Kirov is alleged to have told Stalin that others wanted him to become General Secretary.

◢ The circumstances of Kirov's death are suspicious. Nikolaev, the assassin, was able to gain access to Kirov's Leningrad offices despite having been arrested previously for stalking him. Some writers claim that the NKVD trained him.

◢ Nikolaev was speedily interrogated and shot while the guards associated with his arrest rapidly perished, taking their secrets with them.

◢ Emergency powers against terrorism were rapidly approved and a wave of arrests and executions followed. These may have been prepared beforehand.

◢ The assassination was used to legitimise the trials and repression from 1936.

◢ Most of the delegates to the 1934 Congress were dead by 1938 as Stalin remade the Party on the basis of loyalty to himself.

1934 Party Congress delegates: 1,966   Alive 5 years later: 798
1934 Central Committee members: 139   Alive 5 years later: 41

The case against rejects most of the above points as circumstantial

◢ Kirov was not a liberal. He was a hard, opportunistic Party boss in a similar mould to Stalin. Trotsky called him the 'unscrupulous Leningrad dictator'.

◢ There is no direct evidence of a rift between the two men. They worked closely together and Zhdanov, who replaced Kirov, continued similar policies. Kirov may have clashed with Kaganovich, but if there was a major rift in the Politburo, it was between Molotov and Ordzhonikidze.

◢ It is possible that the NKVD organised the killing. Borisov, Kirov's bodyguard, had a fatal accident before Stalin could interrogate him. It is also possible that Nikolaev acted alone.

◢ There is no real pattern to the immediate arrests and most of those executed were ex-White Guards, rather than Bolsheviks. This suggests a panicking leadership striking out blindly in retaliation against what it feared was a genuine plot. The emergency powers against Terrorism were rarely used.

◢ Despite most show trial defendants being accused of involvement in the murder, those arrested in late 1935 were not shot until after a second trial in 1936, while Radek and Bukharin were considered trustworthy enough to be allowed to draft the 1936 Constitution. This suggests that the Kirov link was not critical to their deaths.

◢ Much of the evidence is based on 'confessions' in the Show Trials or on the hearsay evidence of Orlov and Nicolaevski (see chapter 6), neither of whom were in Russia at the time. Their version only appeared after 1953. Its reliability is highly questionable. Neither Trotsky nor Khrushchev blamed Stalin.

The Moscow Show Trials

The most extraordinary events of the late 1930s were the trials of Old Bolshevik leaders. Attacked by prosecutor Vyshinski, many of them confessed to fantastic crimes and conspiracies and were duly executed. Some were acquitted, only to be recharged when their colleagues had incriminated them. None of these men held real power, so they presented little threat to Stalin but almost all were killed. Their fate provides the most persuasive case that Stalin planned the Purges. Bukharin blamed Stalin's 'morbid suspiciousness' for their deaths.

In the summer of 1936, the Kirov case was reopened with Kamenev, Zinoviev and others described as 'Trotskyists', accused of political crimes, including assassination. Possibly this derives from the belated discovery of Trotsky's 'network', but equally likely it relates to a power-struggle within the NKVD between Yagoda and his deputy, EZHOV. Although few in power were threatened by the trial and execution of the 'Leftists', increasing calls for vigilance were heard.

The Kemerovo mine explosion of September 1936 was blamed on sabotage. Almost immediately, Ezhov replaced Yagoda and launched a hunt for conspirators. One result was the trial of 'Trotskyists', including Radek and Piatakov, in January 1937. Piatakov was Ordzhonikidze's deputy and his conviction demonstrated that enemies had penetrated every level within the bureaucracy. Divisions between moderates and radicals in the Politburo were now critical, having failed to prevent Piatakov's execution, Ordzhonikidze shot himself.

Profile NARKOM EZHOV   1895–1940

Originally a metalworker in a Petrograd arms factory, Ezhov (see Figure 19) was drafted but deserted from the Tsar's Army and joined the Bolsheviks in 1917, playing an active role in the Revolution. He served as a military commissar against guerrillas after the Civil War and played an enthusiastic role in collectivisation. Under Kaganovich's patronage, he rose through the Party administration, gaining a reputation for loyalty and discipline. His biographer, Starkov, describes him as a 'colourless, mediocre individual', but he was devoted to Stalin and suspicious of those from bourgeois backgrounds. Within the NKVD he investigated the Kirov Murder. He also wrote a book which equated faction with counter-revolution and developed the theory of a

Figure 19 Narkom Ezhov, the NKVD boss. Should he, rather than Stalin, be held responsible for the violence of 1936–8?

Zinoviev–Trotskyite conspiracy. As NKVD boss, he organised the trials of Old Bolsheviks, the Army Purge and the Vigilance Campaign. He was capable of fabricating evidence; in fact he faked an assassination attempt against himself. He also set his police quotas for arrests. By 1938 he had alienated many in the Politburo and they turned on him. Shifted to Water Transport, he did not have to wait long before his own arrest and subsequent execution. The charge was 'Leftist over-reaction'.

Defendants in the Trotskyite trial implicated former 'Rightist' leaders in their plots. After an earlier acquittal, Bukharin found himself facing capital charges in 1938. His fellow 'conspirators' included Rykov and the deposed police chief, Yagoda. Tomsky had cheated Stalin by shooting himself. Fitzroy Maclean's account of Stalin secretly watching the trial reinforces the idea that he was personally responsible. However, it is equally easy to blame Ezhov. There is insufficient evidence to prove either case. Naturally, this case captured world attention. Bukharin admitted responsibility, but skilfully defended himself on the specific charges but his co-defendants accused him and they were all shot. Why people confessed has always been a matter for discussion. Some were clearly tortured while others surrendered in return for safeguards about their families or because in some way they felt that their deaths would help the USSR survive, however badly led.

The Army Purge: June 1937

Despite an increasing threat from Germany, 1937 saw the execution without trial of most of the military leadership. Many sources report 50 per cent of the Officer Corps shot, although recent research by Reese has revised the proportion downwards as the Red Army was larger than realised and because many of those arrested were later reinstated.

Incredibly, Marshal Tukhachevsky and his colleagues were supposed to have plotted to betray Russia to the Nazis and launch a coup against Stalin. While some documents were produced to support the former, these are likely to have been Gestapo or NKVD forgeries. Army leaders had expressed some concerns about the events of 1936–7 and several had criticised Stalin's comrade, Defence Chief Voroshilov. However, there is no direct evidence of a plot. So unlikely was their disloyalty that this affair is easily construed as evidence of Stalin's paranoia. The military still enjoyed considerable autonomy and perhaps Stalin wanted to ensure political control of them. Many of the top officers were opposed to a deal with Germany (see chapter 6), but this seems insufficient reason to kill them. The real reasons remain a mystery although the affair certainly stoked the fires of the *Ezhovchina*.

The *Ezhovchina* and the wider purge

Most of those killed in 1937–8 were neither Old Bolsheviks nor military officers. By mid-1937, a number of processes came together to create what John Arch-Getty terms 'a maelstrom of political violence' and which other writers have seen as an irrational killing spree.

◢ The Stakhanovite Movement created tension between workers and managers, with plenty of accusations of obstruction or sabotage. Certainly, scapegoats were sought as Industry ran into problems.

◢ Within the Party, the verification and exchange of documents hit an impasse as local officials blocked or ignored it. Zhdanov's reaction, which Stalin backed, was to promote 'vigilance' by encouraging criticism of Party bureaucracy. Zhdanov hoped this would make the April 1937 elections meaningful and remove poor leaders. While turnover was around 50 per cent in the elections, most cliques with real power remained in post.

◢ Despite Stalin's call to avoid a witch-hunt, Ezhov's NKVD continued to pursue class enemies. The Army Plot seemed to be the fuse which lit the powder-keg. Suddenly, bad Party work or bureaucratism was seen as 'wrecking', just as incompetence or errors were in industry. Wrecking, in the frenzied climate of 1937, was treason. When the police swooped on regional and party officials, evidence of 'nests' or 'families' and of bribery, hoarding and falsification of reports was easily uncovered. These were not part of a Trotskyite conspiracy, but their existence was enough to convict their members. Those arrested were then encouraged to implicate others. Under pressure to demonstrate its vigilance by unmasking enemies, the NKVD issued arrest quotas to its officers.

◢ As ordinary people continued to criticise and denounce those above them, abuse became rife and events ran out of control. Stalin declared that grumblers were enemies, while the NKVD began to reward informers with a share of their victim's property. People used denunciation to settle scores and eliminate rivals for jobs or housing, or simply to get their denunciation in first. Other leaders used the Purges to remove followers of rivals from their agencies. To ensure truculent republics were brought to heel, senior politicians were dispatched to purge them. The Ukraine suffered particularly severely from the visits of Khrushchev.

◢ Reasons for arrest and execution became increasingly bizarre. When Army horses died, their stablehands were shot as German agents. The horses actually died because of a fungus which grew on wet fodder. Jews were even accused of working for the Nazis to set up a fascist government! Not only Soviet citizens died. Poles, Germans and Spaniards were among foreign Communists arrested and shot while living in exile in Moscow. At its most grotesque, children were rewarded for denouncing their parents.

End of the Purges

By late 1937, the scale of killings threatened to destabilise the regime by eliminating those required to manage it. The embarrassing 1937 Census had to be suppressed. Imprisonment increasingly replaced execution as punishment and criticism emerged of the excesses committed by 'overvigilant careerists' in the NKVD. Censured by the

Politburo in December, Ezhov was demoted and replaced by BERIA. Beria then eliminated much of the leadership of the NKVD who had been 'infiltrated' by 'Trotskyites'. Those who knew the truth were soon dead. As the violence was wound down, a new Party recruitment drive allowed back many who had survived expulsion.

Profile LAVRENTI BERIA 1899–1953

A Georgian and second generation Stalinist, Beria worked in intelligence and then in the Party in the Caucasus. He rose to prominence by producing a sycophantic account of Stalin as a Georgian Revolutionary and by denouncing his own boss, Eunikidze. Put in charge of the NKVD, he eliminated Ezhov and other senior officers. He went on to carve out a security empire during the Civil War and acquired a reputation for cruelty and arrogance. After Zhdanov's death he seemed likely to succeed Stalin. However, the other leaders feared him and he was executed shortly after Stalin's death.

Who were the victims?

Most historical research has focused on the trials of earlier leaders. This provides ammunition for the idea of Stalin as vengeful and paranoid, as do studies which have noted the casualty rate among Congress delegates from 1934. Having recast the Party since 1928 in alliance with a first generation of 'Stalinists', did Stalin use his own 'Night of the Long Knives' to create a second generation including Zhdanov, Malenkov, Beria and Khrushchev? These men would be loyal and subservient to him, rather than seeing themselves as collective leaders. There are also some deaths where it is difficult to see anything but personal hatred as the motive; for example, Eunikidze and Trotsky.

The logic of the personal motive for the Purges starts to break down when one considers the wider bloodlettings. Stalin, while responsible overall and personally signing many death warrants in a day, cannot have heard of more than a fraction of his victims; virtually none of whom constituted a threat to him. Around one in 18 of the population were arrested at some point. Many of them would have considered themselves his loyal supporters. Of 2.8 million Party members in 1934, 1 million were arrested and over 60% of these executed. Overall deaths are discussed in chapter 5, but probably exceeded a million.

Despite the focus in books and films on artists and intellectuals, they were more likely to be restricted than executed. Vulnerability analysis, which relates categories of victims to their numbers in the population as a whole, shows that while 90 per cent of gulag inmates were peasants, Party officials were hardest hit. Trapped between Zhdanov's democratic criticism campaigns from below and Ezhov's vigilance from above, the bureaucracy was decimated. The most vulnerable were high ranking office-holders in the military, Party or economy, particularly those who had been in opposition. This has been supported by regional studies, although there are other variables (*e.g.* Hiroaki Kuromiya's Donbas study revealed increases in arrests whenever Kaganovich visited, which suggests another personal factor).

Understanding the Purges

The question 'What were the purges?' is as important as 'why?' in getting to grips with these events. Since there were a range of different processes at work, which somehow meshed to create the killings, a range of different causes was probably at work.

Although it is possible to construct a case around Stalin's devastation at his wife's suicide in 1932 and the Riutin Affair, much of this would be speculation about his personality since there is a lack of primary evidence about his mental state. Similarly, while Russia has a history of autocratic rulers who used arbitrary punishments to ensure their position, that does not prove it happened in the 1930s. Certainly Stalin's experience of the Revolution and Krondstadt might make him feel insecure in a crisis, but there is no evidence of a devilish master plan to eliminate all potential critics. In any case, this explanation raises further questions:

◢ Why did he not exile rather than kill?

◢ Why did he kill so many that it threatened Russia's security?

◢ If he was so powerful, how could there be opposition and why did he need excuses to crush it?

The problems in the Party were to do with quality and obedience rather than political opposition. In the struggle for collectivisation and industrialisation, control of the quality of party membership had been lost. As a result, some didn't even know who the leaders were, let alone what Marxism was. There was also an escalating struggle between

Moscow and regional officials who frustrated the government's initiatives and failed to keep the leadership informed. The struggle with those Stalin described as 'Red Tapists, Old Heroes' and 'honest windbags' obsessed the leadership during the mid-1930s. Many attempts were made to break the impasse and by 1937 Zhdanov and Ezhov, both Stalin's protégés, were initiating separate and contradictory campaigns. Stalin backed both of them, although he ultimately favoured Zhdanov. While Stalin personally despised those he called 'neckties', vigilance and democratisation were supposed to reform the Party bureaucracy, not destroy it. Unfortunately, things got out of control.

The purging of the Party was itself not unusual, but the violence was. This seems to have happened after it became entangled with the charges of counter-revolution and treason made in the Moscow Trials and Army Plot. At a local level, there was corruption but not political subversion. What ensued was thus terror rather than repression, since there was no opposition to repress. According to Gábor Rittersporn, the terror fed on widespread belief in the population of conspiracies which caused hardships and shortages. This is rooted in rural beliefs about malign spirits. If the people were willing to believe in conspiracies and the NKVD were looking for them, it is easy to see how the Terror developed. Many individuals contributed to its growth. At the top, senior politicians and Ezhov; below them, the NKVD; and below them, the hordes of citizens who informed and denounced those around them. Despite Stalin's instructions, events bear striking resemblance to witch-crazes from earlier centuries.

Effects of the Purges

Some of the effects are self-evident, but Figure 20 indicates the diverse impact these events had on the USSR.

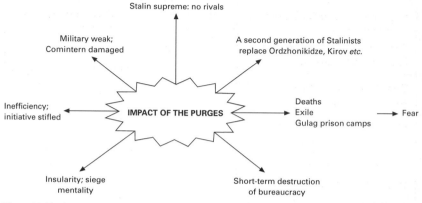

Figure 20 The impact of the Purges

TASKS

1 Dealing with many conflicting accounts can be confusing. Gather your ideas together by drawing up a grid or table in order to compare possible explanations with the evidence.

Explanation and key writers	Evidence for	Evidence against
Stalin planned the Purges (Deutscher, Fainsod)		
The Purges result from Stalin's irrationality or paranoia (Tucker, Medvedev)		
The Purges derive from Lenin and Communism (Arendt, Shapiro, Conquest)		
There was opposition . . . (Shapiro, Bullock)		
They should be seen as reactions . . . (Lewin, Acton, Nove)		
Other leaders and agencies helped create and shape 'the Purges' (Arch-Getty, Manning, Rittersporn)		
The Purges took on a life of their own (Brezinski, Cohen)		

(Note: several of these statements overlap and writers may hold several of these positions simultaneously.)

2 Historiographical questions

Increasingly, exam boards are devoting questions or entire papers to considering debates among historians and the nature of their evidence.

They require you to demonstrate an awareness that history is constructed from imperfect evidence and to be able to identify how and why writers differ. The example below is fairly typical, but before you answer it, read chapter 6.

Did Stalin plan The Purges?

Read through the sources, then answer the questions which follow.

◢ Source A

The shadow of the last Tsar must have more than once appeared before Stalin, as he viewed Hitler's preliminaries to war. One might sketch an imaginary conversation between the living man and the ghost. 'Your end is approaching,' the phantom whispers. 'Remember the terrible turmoil in Petersburg when the news came that the Germans had captured Riga? What if the Germans appear in Riga again, or in Kiev, or at the gates of Moscow?' 'You had the formidable Bolshevik Party against you, while I have exiled Trotsky and crushed all my other opponents.' The phantom roars with laughter: 'In 1914–17 did I not keep you in Siberia and were not Lenin and Trotsky in exile? . . .'

No milder pretext for the slaughter of the old guard would have sufficed. Had they been executed merely as men opposed to Stalin or even as conspirators who had tried to remove him from power, many might still have regarded them as martyrs for a good cause. They had to die as traitors, as perpetrators of crimes beyond the reach of reason, as leaders of a monstrous fifth column. Only then could Stalin be sure that their execution would provoke no dangerous revulsion; and that, on the contrary, he himself would be looked upon, especially by the young and uninformed generation, as the saviour of the country.

Isaac Deutscher, **Stalin** *(OUP, 1949)*

◢ Source B

(The 1934 Congress) became Stalin's final estrangement from the Bolshevik Party. Instead of being reassured of his unique place in party esteem and fully converted to the reconciliation line, he became more embittered, solitary, vengeful and dangerous. If his will to vengeance had softened with the passage of time . . . it must have hardened now. If he had wavered before in his belief that the Party was honeycombed with enemies scheming against him, he could do so no longer. Now he knew that treason was rife even in the Party's highest organ of authority, the Congress.

... In the aftermath of the congress experience, what seemed necessary was not simply a continuation of the operation that had been going on in recent months but a purge of a new kind – new in scope and in method. Not a bloodless weeding out as in the past but a purge in which expulsion would mean repression as a traitorous enemy of the Revolution; and not a mere diminution of numbers but a radical renovation of the Party undertaken as the next big task of the revolution from above. A whole generation of Party members who had failed the test of fealty must go, their places to be taken by a new generation of 'real Bolsheviks' who would fail the test ... Let a party of Lenin–Stalin worshippers be created.

Robert Tucker, **Stalin in Power** *(Norton, 1992)*

◢ Source C

An understanding of the thirties based on Stalin's personality is as limiting and incomplete as an explanation of Nazism derived primarily from Hitler's psyche ... A chaotic local bureaucracy, a quasi-feudal network of politicians accustomed to arresting people and a set of perhaps insoluble political and social problems created an atmosphere conducive to violence. All it took from Stalin were catalytic and probably ad hoc interventions. The evidence suggests that the Ezhovchina should be redefined. It was not the result of a petrified bureaucracy stamping out dissent and annihilating old radical revolutionaries ... the Ezhovchina was a radical, even hysterical, reaction to bureaucracy. Officeholders were destroyed from above and below in a chaotic wave of voluntarism and revolutionary puritanism.

John Arch-Getty, **Origins of the Great Purges** *(UUP, 1985)*

◢ Source D

As he'd got older my father had begun feeling lonely. He was so isolated from everyone that he seemed to be living in a vacuum. He hadn't a soul he could talk to. It was the system of which he himself was a prisoner and in which he was stifling from emptiness and lack of human companionship.

Alliluyeva Stalin *(Stalin's daughter)*

◢ Source E

... it was at that very period, between the murder of Kirov and the second Kamenev Trial, that Stalin made his decision and mapped out his plan of 'reforms'... The determining reason for Stalin's decision was his realisation, arrived at on the basis of reports and information reaching him, that the mood of the majority of the old Party

workers was really one of bitterness and hostility towards him ... *As Stalin perceived it, the reasons for the hostility towards him lay in the* basic psychology of the old Bolsheviks. *Having grown up under the conditions of revolutionary struggle against the old regime, we had all been trained in the psychology of oppositionists, of irreconcilable nonconformists ...*

The conclusion he (Stalin) drew from all this was certainly daring: if the old Bolsheviks, the group constituting today the ruling caste in the country, are unfit to perform this function, it is necessary to remove them from their posts, to create a new ruling caste.

Bukharin to Nicolaevski in 1936, reported in 'Letter of an Old Bolshevik' (1938)

a What is meant by 'the terrible turmoil in Petersburg' and the 'old guard' in source A?

b How far do sources A and B agree on the reasons for the purge?

c Which of sources A and B could make most use of source D as supporting evidence?

d What problems might the author of source C have with source E?

e In what way does source C disagree with sources A and B about whether the Purges were planned?

f Explain why source C differs from sources A and B?

g Why do historians continue to disagree about the reasons for the Purges?

CHAPTER FIVE

WINNERS AND LOSERS

Objectives
◢ To look at the impact of Stalin's Revolution on Soviet society
◢ To explain why Stalin remained popular despite the terror.

Understanding Soviet society

Amid famine, terror, collectivisation and war, it is difficult to imagine any Soviet citizen gaining from Stalin's revolution, let alone supporting him. We could ascribe his popularity to Soviet 'brainwashing', but this should be thoroughly questioned before we accept it. Implicit in it is the idea that the Russians were somehow less clever or perceptive than we are. Although propagandists would have us believe in the power of their media, the main reasons for continued support may be more mundane. In the complex events of the 1930s most people's social position changed even if they remained in one place. Not everyone faced the terrors of the Gulags and many took the chance of upward social mobility which Stalin's reforms offered them.

Social transformation

With the defeat of the *kulaks*, none of the 'class conflicts' which Marx had identified remained. Nevertheless, it was not a classless society. Stalin identified two classes: workers and peasants, plus a stratum of intellectuals and white-collar workers. Since Communism had not been achieved yet, the State was to remain rather than wither away and be used to create the right conditions for a new type of citizen, loyal to the proletariat and patriotic towards the USSR, to emerge. Stalin's revolution was about social and cultural change as much as about defeating the Rightists and launching industrialisation.

Social policy

The 1930s saw the State zigzag between placating and oppressing the people. As with the economy and politics, decisions made in Moscow often unleashed forces which proved difficult to control and results which were not those the leadership desired. In some respects therefore, changes were initiated or shaped 'from below.'

Utopian Communism (1928–32)

The economic 'left turn' boosted 'Leftist' ideas. Enthusiastic radicals seized the opportunity to complete the Bolshevik Revolution by destroying 'bourgeois institutions'. Attempts were made to replace the legal system with 'comradely courts' and campaigns of 'self-criticism'. In the social sphere, Alexandra Kollontai and others continued to erode families (which distracted workers from building Socialism) by making divorce easier. Militants from the atheist 'League of the Godless' joined police actions against traditionalist peasants during collectivisation. Mosques were closed, icons smashed and priests exiled or killed. Educationalists led by Anatoli Lunacharski campaigned against elitist, academic education. Others attempted 'de-schooling' and then 'learning through labour'. Universities and schools were disrupted and teachers or academics of 'alien origins' persecuted.

Retreat to authoritarianism (1932–4)

Stalin tolerated radical attempts to create a proletarian culture because they helped him defeat the Right, but their campaigns were disruptive. Chaos in schools, Moslem revolts and social problems in the towns multiplied. Widespread accounts exist of drunkenness, brawling and robberies. The press reported prostitution, drug dealing and estates where criminal gangs were in control. 1932–3 saw measures to impose discipline on citizens, including internal passports and draconian labour laws. After 1934 social policy became increasingly conservative.

- Vyshinsky strengthened the legal system as the coercive instrument of the 'united will of the people' as determined by the Party.

- Alarmed by figures from Moscow showing divorce ending one in three marriages and 2.7 abortions for every birth, measures were taken to bolster the family. Homosexuality and incest were recriminalised, abortion virtually banned and divorce made more difficult. Propaganda was used to promote a cult of motherhood.

- While atheist propaganda continued, the pressure on religion subsided and around 45 per cent of the population remained believers. During the Second World War, orthodox Christianity would be promoted again as a symbol of national unity.

Stalinist culture

Bukharin saw no threat from non-Party artists and had allowed these 'fellow travellers' to flourish under NEP. The late 1920s, however, saw attacks by militants, led by the Russian Association of Proletarian Writers (RAPP), against bourgeois influences and artists. While they served a purpose for Stalin, their work was generally too avant garde for the tastes of ordinary citizens. In 1932 RAPP was dissolved and artists ordered to glorify industrialisation and collectivisation in accessible ways. Under *'Socialist realism'*, Stalin urged writers to become 'engineers of human souls' and to assist in constructing Communism. The prototype was Sholokov's trilogy of peasant life, including *Quiet flows the Don*. Zhdanov insisted that apolitical art was by definition bourgeois. Artists who would not conform were accused of Trotskyite or nationalist deviation. Political correctness stifled artistic expression. Shostakovich and Eisenstein found it difficult to work; the poet Mayakovsky killed himself; the playwright Meyerhold and writer Mandelstam died in the gulags.

Stalin's own taste increasingly defined what was acceptable. Architecture was dominated by massive stone and concrete buildings known as 'Stalinist Baroque' which celebrated the permanence of Soviet civilisation (see Figure 21). The palatial Moscow Metro and the capital's administrative buildings epitomise this elaborate style.

KEY TERM

'Socialist realism' embraced civil war 'Westerns', novels with titles like *Cement*, and fairy stories featuring proletarian heroes successfully overcoming obstacles and enemies in all areas of life under the guidance of the Party and inspired by Stalin. Artists were to depict the truth according to the Party. Art was to be entertaining, with strong plots, clear distinctions between heroes and villains and positive messages rather than the internal tensions of much early Soviet writing.

Socialist heroes

In the 1930s, 'hero cults' were promoted which included non-communists. Attempts to develop patriotism involved celebrating earlier rulers and artists such as Prince Nevsky, Pushkin and General Kutuzov. Stalin was very fond of the writer Maxim Gorky and his own idols: Tsars Ivan the Terrible and Peter the Great. Most of these were

Russians and the late 1930s saw the re-imposition of Russian culture (**Russification**) on the other Republics.

Ditching Bolshevik dislike of competition, sport was used to provide symbols of success. Huge stadia were built and sports ranging from horseracing to mountaineering were encouraged. The secret police had their own 'Dynamo' teams, as did the Army (CSKA Moscow) and major industrial concerns (Lokomotiv *etc.*). It was so serious that Beria jailed the Moscow Spartak manager and key players who beat Moscow Dynamo in the 1938 Championship for 10 years.

KEY TERM

Russification – under the Tsars, a main strategy for dominating their multi-ethnic empire was to attempt to turn their subjects into Russians by suppressing all other cultures. Within the USSR, Marxism was supposed to provide the cement. However, old prejudices die hard and even non-Russians such as Stalin became infected with Russian chauvinism once in control. This was more than patriotic pride in things Russian. Chauvinism involves an assumption of Russian superiority and a violent intolerance and suspicion of anything 'alien'.

The cult of Stalin

The leading hero was Stalin. From his fiftieth birthday celebrations in 1929, his image as genius and leader was continually embellished. Artists competed for favour by promoting his achievements in poems, statues and public festivals. History books were rewritten to show his dominant role in the Revolution and Civil War. At a lower level there were Stakhanovites, Young Pioneers and mother heroines who were rewarded for producing children. Across society, awards and honours were distributed to reward loyalty and effort.

The quality of life in the USSR

Housing

As peasants flooded into industrial areas, there was rapid urban growth. New cities, such as Magnitogorsk and Stalinsk, grew from nothing to populations of 169,000 and 146,000 respectively during the 1930s. Existing cities expanded: Sverdlovsk tripled in size and Chelyabinsk quadrupled. The cost of this was chronic overcrowding, squalor and social disorder. People were crammed into barracks,

Figure 21 Proposal for the 'Palace of the Soviets'

factory corridors, mud huts and cellars. Sanitation and other amenities were poor; lice and other insects shared their accommodation.

Living standards

Real wage values are very difficult to assess, but most writers agree that they fell. Shapiro estimated that by the late 1930s they were about half the 1928 levels. More recently, John Barber has provided a picture of a fall to 1933, then stability and improvement before a further decline from 1936. Either way, the early 1930s seem to have been bad. Nove described them as the 'most precipitous peacetime decline in recorded history'. Most families had several members working so household incomes rose, but pooled incomes may have simply enabled them to stand still. Evidence of widespread moonlighting suggests people were having to work harder than before.

Despite fixed prices, the low priority given to consumer goods resulted in shortages. As a result, corruption became universal. 'Blat' (Black market) provided false ration cards, permits and goods when none were available. Most citizens outside the party hierarchy had to construct networks of 'contacts' to survive and to get what they wanted. Similarly, as administration became increasingly bureaucratic contacts and bribes were needed to cut through paperwork. The vulnerability and resentment people felt in this situation is testified to by the support given to anti-corruption purges.

On the other hand, contemporary Western observers claimed that workers were optimistic about the future, were no longer terrified of poverty and were able to have paid holidays for the first time.

Nutrition

Food was in short supply and was rationed from 1929 to 1935. Dairy and meat consumption fell by half; many citizens became almost vegetarian from necessity. Rations were not always met, which meant supplements had to be found for the basic diet of cabbage, potato and rye bread. Stalin advised city dwellers to keep rabbits and to grow mushrooms in their basements. Many did so or took time off work to fish, grow vegetables and barter some little extras. Everyone had to queue for provisions from shops, whose low standards of service became legendary. Nevertheless, despite the famine, the food situation in the towns was less severe than either the last Tsarist years or the civil war period and workers could often buy cheap dinners in factory canteens.

Health and welfare

With depleted diets, health did suffer. Infant mortality rose from the late 1920s and there were epidemics which related to poor nutrition as well as poor conditions. Rickets, in particular, became rife.

However, there were advances. Free medical care was provided and the number of doctors had quadrupled by 1940. The State also provided benefits for those unable to support themselves, although these were reduced in the late 1930s, when maternity leave was cut.

Education

Real progress was made in bringing literacy to virtually all adults, through evening schools, sending teachers to villages and building 70,000 libraries. Workers were educated as specialists and officials, while universities had produced one million graduates by 1940 – one-third of them in engineering. In 1927 most children attended school for four years; by 1940, most attended from 7 to 13. Over 30 per cent of urban children continued to 17, despite the introduction of fees. In quantitative terms this compared favourably with Britain.

From 1934, education became formal and conformist. The progressive methods and anti-academic campaigns of the late 1920s were replaced with a traditional curriculum with only approved material and ideas being studied. Homework, uniforms, exams and discipline returned. History, which had been considered irrelevant after the Revolution, was reinstated. Its role was to promote patriotism and knowledge of world events culminating in the victory of Soviet Communism. Schoolbooks were based on Stalin's single approved text: the 'Short Course'.

Science also suffered from ideology. Stalin's pamphlets on issues such as linguistics and politics could not be contradicted. Geologists who failed to find minerals found themselves on treason charges for deliberately ignoring the nation's wealth. Similarly, when Stalin favoured an idea such as Lysenko's on plant breeding, its alternative became counter-revolutionary and could not be taught. The quality of education suffered from this second wave of disruption and through over-rapid expansion. Graduates were often at little more than secondary school levels.

Employment

There was a huge expansion of specialist jobs, from midwives to engineers. The 1926 Census records only half a million specialists, but by 1939 this had risen to over 12 million, although this non-manual figure includes everyone from Party bosses to shop assistants. The proportion of jobs outside agriculture rose from 20 to 33 per cent in the same period (see Figure 22).

Within the workforce hierarchies began to develop, particularly from 1931 when egalitarianism was denounced as 'anti-Socialist' and differential pay was reintroduced to combat 'flitting'. Those with marketable skills were able to capitalise in both material and status terms. While for many there were ladders, for others there were snakes.

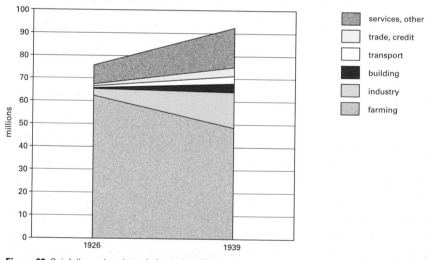

Figure 22 Gainfully employed population in the USSR, by branch, 1926 and 1939 (Source: Wheatcroft and Davies)

The differential impact on the Soviet people

Party members

The Cold War view of Russia was of a system run for the benefit of the Party bosses. Undoubtedly, they were privileged – with cars, pensions and *dachas* (holiday homes) – but they were particularly vulnerable to arrest and execution in the Purges. Despite the risks, numbers rose to over 3 million.

Party membership made promotion more likely, with all the benefits that brought; virtually all managers were members. Party officials themselves (*Apparatchiks*) became a new elite with both power and access to privileges, including special shops and housing. Examination of members suggests that certain groups did better than others.

	Workers	Peasants	Others
1934 Party members origin	60%	8%	32%
1934 Party members actual jobs	9%	2%	89%

While members may have exaggerated proletarian backgrounds or concealed bourgeois ones, it is clear that the Party changed in the 1930s. It became the Party of the bureaucracy, intelligentsia and specialists. By 1940 most of the new recruits came from a white-collar background. The leadership remained apart: only Molotov did not have peasant or working-class origins. This flood of new members tended to be traditionalist and to respect a strong state. They increasingly overlapped with other elite groups at the top of industry and the State. Analysis revealed that certain ethnic groups did better than others. Unsurprisingly, Russians and Georgians did well while Kazakhs and Ukrainians were under-represented. Numbers of Jews in prominent positions declined during the 1930s. Only about 15 per cent of members were women.

The white-collar elite

Initially, the non-Party intellectuals and managers who had been needed to run universities, the bureaucracy and the economy suffered under Stalin. However, after the purges of 'bourgeois specialists', surviving technicians and engineers found themselves much in demand and could command better wages and conditions. As late as 1939, only 12 per cent of State employees were Party members and only 3 per cent of teachers. To these were added newly-trained ex-workers. In 1931, office workers lost their 'bourgeois' stigma and were given equal status with workers. By the mid 1930s Stalin was telling managers' wives to be role models in spreading cleanliness, values and culture to those below them. While these Stalinist 'yuppies' proved vulnerable in the Purges, the possessions, power and respect which accompanied their posts outweighed the dangers. They could afford the secondary school fees to enable their children to join the next generation of leaders. From the War onwards, the Soviet system began to ossify and this new elite consolidated their position. *Apparatchiks* and managers were the biggest winners under Stalin.

Workers

The working class doubled in size in the early 1930s to some 20 million and reached 30 million by 1940, although many of the new jobs were as labourers. The nature of this class changed too. In 1928 most workers had proletarian parents, but by 1933 most were ex-peasants. Through the acquisition of skills and some study it was possible to go from peasant to official inside a generation. Many original workers became *apparatchiks* and many later Soviet leaders, such as Khrushchev, benefited from this meritocracy. Amongst workers, wage differentials widened. Those producing capital goods did better than those in consumer industry. On top of this, there was additional status and privileges for shockworkers or Stakhanovites.

Peasants

Like a defeated people, the peasants suffered greatly. A quarter of families were dekulakised. Perhaps 5–6 million were exiled, many dying along the way or in harsh camps and settlements. Most peasants were at starvation level in 1932, 1933 and 1936. Some areas did worse than others. The Ukraine famine is famous but losses among the Kazakhs of Central Asia were even more dramatic. Nomads herded into farms lost both their way of life and their animals. Many starved, while others fled over the borders. Even if not labelled *kulaks*, peasants were treated as second-class citizens, virtually the property of the *kolkhoz*. They had less rations than workers, were forced to work on roads and prohibited from leaving their farms without permission. Despite this, millions fled to find work in towns. Should we equate progress with their shift from farming to labouring, even if their children would now be educated?

Other dimensions

Class is not the only way to analyse the USSR. Vertical divisions in experience cut across the horizontal bands of classes.

Ethnicity

Stalin saw himself as a national welder in the mode of Ivan the Terrible and his adopted Russian chauvinism was reflected in social policy. Central control of the economy led to tensions with the Republics, such as when the Uzbeks were ordered to grow cotton rather than food. Sovietisation by the mid 1930s became 'Russification'.

Russian was made the official language and Cyrillic the approved script. Ironically, literacy encouraged a revival of local cultures and many local Communists exhibited pride in their own national traditions. This made them suspect in Stalin's eyes. Muslim Party members were particularly vulnerable in this respect, often resisting 'modernisation' such as the removal of women's veils and the banning of polygamy. A spate of risings were crushed and non-Russian elites were purged. Mass arrests of 'bourgeois nationalist' leaders and intellectuals followed, many of them being executed. They were replaced by loyal Communists, usually Russians. Against this repression should be set the location of industry in many undeveloped areas, which brought the prospect of advancement for some.

Gender

Women in towns found employment easy to come by. Forty per cent of new workers in the early 1930s were women, who moved beyond their traditional areas of textiles and light industry into most occupations. By 1939 they made up 43 per cent of all workers and were a majority in the Moscow proletariat. Women workers tended to be younger and more inexperienced than their male counterparts and few reached the top in any fields but they did have full rights as citizens, and held many posts which remained male-dominated in the West.

Women workers as a percentage of total workforce

	Britain	USSR
Mining	0.6	24
Engineering	5.4	23.4
Textiles	54.2	70.1
Construction	1.2	19

(Source: Barber and Davies)

The restrictions on abortion and divorce were not accompanied by a drive to return women to the home. On the contrary, women were still expected to have a full public life and officials tended to back women in disputes about their rights. The impact of this was particularly strong in Islamic regions. Propaganda still celebrated women achievers who had escaped traditionalist husbands, women's football teams coexisted with homemaker magazines. It was a complex 'dual role'.

Age

The urban workforce was young. By 1932, 40 per cent of miners were under 23 as were most of the workers at the new tractor factories in Kharkov and Stalingrad. The young were a particular focus for Communist propaganda. Most children were enroled in the Young Pioneer or *Komsomol* organisations (see Figure 23) to ensure a constant supply of enthusiasts for radical change. Whether this reflects the indoctrination of the young or genuine idealism is difficult to assess.

Victims

There are also disparities when it comes to identifying losers. Party officials and urban areas may have suffered hardest in the Purges, but the countryside bore the brunt of the famine and deportations. In 1932–3, peasants were denied passports to prevent them sharing the meagre rations allocated to the towns. The Party remained true to its roots in this respect: it was still the party of the proletariat.

Prisoners

At the bottom of the heap were the prisoners in the network of prison camps, labour colonies and fenced 'special settlements': the 'Gulag Archipelago'. Harsh or freezing conditions, insufficient food and brutal regimes made their lives unbearable. Unsurprisingly, vast numbers died, while many of the largely innocent inmates had their lives

СПАСИБІ ПАРТІЇ,
СПАСИБІ РІДНОМУ СТАЛІНУ
ЗА ЩАСЛИВЕ, ВЕСЕЛЕ
ДИТИНСТВО.

Figure 23 This 1937 Grinets poster translates as *Thanks to the Party, Thanks to Dear Stalin for a Happy Joyful Childhood*. Children were encouraged to revere Stalin as a benevolent father figure as his cult hit new heights in the 1930s

destroyed. Just how many citizens were affected has been fiercely debated. Conquest, and some post-Soviet sources have estimated that over 20 million passed through the camps with 7–8 million in the years 1937–8 alone. Wheatcroft's recent study of Soviet statistics challenges these since they imply that nearly half of all men between 30 and 60 were incarcerated. Wheatcroft argues that the real figures are less than half of those given by Conquest, with perhaps 3 million imprisoned in 1938–9.

'Excess deaths'

A macabre debate has taken place about the numbers who perished during Stalin's Revolution. Cold War accounts put famine victims in excess of 10 million, with up to 10–20 million dying in the camps. The period is a demographer's nightmare. Until recently, the 1937 census was suppressed and historians doubted the reliability of the 1939 figures. This meant that they used the 1926 and 1955 censuses and then estimated birth and death rates from accounts of ex-prisoners, local sources and partial Soviet material. Their task was complicated by deaths in the 1941–5 War. Again, recent research has tended to reduce these totals considerably. Wheatcroft's study of the 1937 census reveals that some 8 million previously thought dead had survived, while his estimates of executions and camp deaths in the key years of 1937–8 as 0.6–1.5 million contradict Conquest's figures of 3–3.5 million. As with most other debates about Stalin, it revolves around the weight and validity given by historians to incomplete or contradictory sources. As a minimum, it seems that at least 20 million suffered some form of serious repression under Stalin.

The end of the Cold War has removed some of the propaganda value of these figures so there may be more chance of consensus in the future.

Explaining control

Officially, Soviet citizens supported Communist policies and revered Stalin as a god. This view is no longer accepted as sufficient explanation for apparent consent. The Totalitarian model of the USSR is based on the theory that the State manipulated and controlled its citizens, which explains the lack of resistance. It did this in two ways:

1 'Massification' involved indoctrinating citizens with Communist Party ideology through control of the media, censorship and cultural products. The existence of these messages is easy to show, as is the network of spies and informers who enforced it. However, oral histories tend to support the argument that people espoused 'correct' views in public and had other thoughts at home.

2 'Atomisation' involved smashing the non-Communist institutions between State and individuals and replacing them with Soviet models. According to Service, Stalin came very close to dissolving society. No intermediate groups were tolerated, private clubs and printing presses were closed. Activities involving foreign connections, such as speaking Esperanto or stamp collecting invited arrest. However, by 1933 social disintegration threatened economic success and the State began a process of reinforcing key institutions such as the family.

Revisionist historians have tended to dismiss Totalitarian models as not being founded on evidence and have begun to produce studies of resistance which undermine the notion of an all-powerful state. They point to other factors which enabled the Party to rule. Gábor Rittersporn identifies two groups whose conflict dominated the 1930s: those who supported the regime through self-interest and the disorganised masses who they had to get to work.

Unpacking a concept

Zhdanov defined 'Socialist realism' as follows:

Its basic subject matter (is) the life of the working class and the peasantry and their struggle for socialism... the main heroes are the active builders of the new life – workers and collective farmers, Komsomols, Pioneers... It must be able... to see our tomorrow (which) is being prepared... today.

a Find an example from each of music, architecture, art and literature. You could use some of the illustrations in this book as starting-points.

b Analyse each using a star diagram (like Figure 24) to determine how useful the label 'Socialist realism' is.

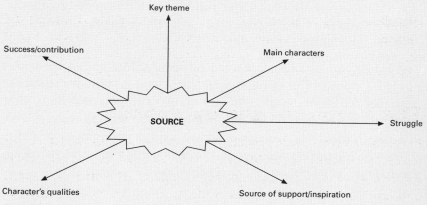

Figure 24

CHAPTER SIX

STALIN AND THE VERDICT OF HISTORY: WHY IS THE JURY STILL OUT?

Objectives

◢ To determine the basis of the historical debate about Stalin
◢ To decide how we can deal with the sources in this debate.

There is a lot of historical writing on Soviet Russia, with Stalin featuring as hero, villain or madman and both creator and creation of the Soviet system. That system has been depicted either as a disciplined machine or as ramshackle and chaotic.

Historians differ in their selection of evidence. There is also rivalry between them. However, the gulf in writing on Stalin is so wide that it can only be comprehended by reflecting on the nature of the sources and the contexts and perspectives of the historians themselves.

The nature of the evidence

Problems of access to, and reliability of, sources were particularly acute for researchers into Soviet history prior to *Glasnost*. In a society where information was propaganda official documents are suspect. Economic data, as chapter 3 described, was created rather than collected. In addition, there is little in the way of personal correspondence or diaries kept by the leadership. Perhaps none existed. Much was not recorded or did not survive the War. It also seems that leaders, reared on secrecy, destroyed embarrassing or incriminating documents.

The flawed and partial nature of available sources makes the reconstruction of decision-making particularly difficult. Official speeches, directives, statistics and newspapers are obviously tainted, so may not provide reliable reasons for events. However, they provide insights into what the concerns of the leadership were and what they wanted done. Stalin's own views are problematic because his speeches were often (deliberately?) ambivalent.

Defectors such as Orlov (NKVD) or Kritvisky (military intelligence) wrote about Stalin's decisions yet neither was in close touch with the leaders or even in the USSR during the periods they are used for. They also had a personal interest in providing whatever pleased their new masters, e.g. US intelligence. Others like the engineer Kravchenko provide insight into particular experiences, but not decision-making.

Many Russian émigrés (exiles) besides Trotsky published memoirs. Some are partly works of propaganda, while others, such as Nicolaevski's 'Letters of an Old Bolshevik', contain inaccuracies and may simply be collections of anti-Stalinist rumour. None of their works are first-hand accounts of the Politburo in the 1930s.

Many Western visitors to the USSR were Communist sympathisers. Some like Scott were enthusiasts who helped develop industries. They provide insights into what went on, but not why. Others, such as Sidney and Beatrice Webb, were given guided tours of the 'new civilisation'. They travelled during the Famine but failed to see any evidence of it. Writers with diplomatic backgrounds, such as Fitzroy Maclean in *Eastern Approaches* (1991), reveal something of espionage and security issues, but not into the real workings of the system.

Data was gathered by Western military intelligence, but whatever was released was carefully selected. The US Army also captured the Smolensk Area Party archives from the Nazis who had looted them in 1941. They provide evidence about the state of Soviet organisation in one region but aside from Fainsod's study they were under-exploited until recently.

After 1956, Khrushchev released some state documents but these were carefully chosen to support his policy changes. They may not be typical or comprehensive. Dissident writers provide valuable accounts of the experience of those repressed, but since they were dissidents they would not be privy to the leadership's thoughts.

The development of historical writing on Stalin

Before 1953

Within the USSR only one version of history was permitted. 'The Short Course', published from 1938, established Stalin as the loyal follower of Lenin and architect of military and industrial victory. Amended as leaders rose and fell from grace, its essence remained constant and it was the basis for Soviet textbooks.

Figure 25 Poster by G Klucis. 'Raise the banner of Lenin and Stalin' (1937)

Much of this was by political scientists rather than historians, and they focused on the leadership, Party structures and ideology and neglected the impact of social, cultural and economic forces.

Trotsky, from exile, welcomed industrialisation but attacked the victory of bureaucracy over Communism. His *Revolution Betrayed* (1973) depicts Stalin as a mediocrity who became 'gravedigger of the Revolution'. Trotsky's work was essentially propaganda, offering a non-Stalinist version of Communism. Nevertheless, many writers treated Trotsky as an authoritative source on the events of the 1930s.

After 1945, Western left-wing writers hailed Soviet economic achievements. Deutscher said Stalin's excesses were tempered by his foresight in ensuring loyalty and successfully industrialising in order to defeat Fascism. E. H. Carr's more traditional Marxist work focuses on economic and political forces although he still sees Stalin as a strong dictator.

Cold War accounts

As the USSR became the West's principle enemy, research proliferated. While much was driven by a desire to understand the new superpower, it also served a political purpose. Comparisons were drawn between the USSR and Nazi Germany. This benefited politicians, industrialists and generals concerned to mobilise public support for the expense and sacrifice of the Cold War. Some research was sponsored by the US military. From Arendt's model of Totalitarianism, through Shapiro's analysis, to Conquest's detailed accounts of the terror, many assumptions are shared: Communism was a system where a dictatorship exercised control through Party and State, ruthlessly eliminating its opponents and terrorising the population. The historian's role was to show how they did it. Conquest took this to its logical conclusion in depicting the Famine as deliberate policy. Most of these writers relied heavily on émigrés and defectors as sources.

Khrushchev's version of Soviet history in 1959 reinforced Western views. The USSR was disciplined and the Party was in control, but Stalin and Ezhov had abused this power. This account was self-serving in that it legitimised Khrushchev's new direction while omitting his role in the Ukrainian Purge. He maintained this line in his autobiography *Khrushchev Remembers* (1971). Under Brezhnev from 1964 there was a swing back towards Stalin, but a can of worms had been opened. Unofficial 'dissident' or 'Samizdat' histories developed Khrushchev's critique of Stalin. Solzhenitsin's novels went further, condemning Communism as a Totalitarian disaster for Russia. His books became popular in the West, but while their literary qualities are undoubted, his works are polemics, not histories.

Revisionism and *Glasnost*

The first cracks in the Totalitarian paradigm came when historians steered away from high politics and abandoned assumptions about the Soviet system. Economic historians such as Alec Nove explored the way policy fluctuated in reaction to the problems of industrialisation rather than following a clear master plan. Moshe Lewin's social studies continued to blame Stalin but also showed the roles of the Party, government agencies and Russian peasant society in shaping events. Lewin doesn't see himself as a revisionist, but his works first exposed the chaotic nature of events, particularly during collectivisation.

From the 1970s research fragmented. Taking their cue from Lewin, historians explored previously neglected sources in a kaleidoscope of social and local histories as well as biographical research into secondary figures. While many reject the catch-all label 'revisionist school of history', these new accounts share a multicausal approach to explaining the past. In focusing on the structure they tend to reveal tension, conflict and pressure from below, rather than passivity. Taken collectively, the work of Roberta Manning, Sheila Fitzpatrick, Lynne Viola and others, results in a chaotic model of the USSR, with Stalin struggling to achieve his fluctuating goals.

John Arch-Getty and Gábor Rittersporn are the most widely known. Their accounts of the Purges explode the intentionalist model. They are also vitriolic in their attacks on earlier historians for sloppiness in ignoring evidence and uncritically accepting rumour and speculation. They see the Totalitarian Model as convenient to Trotskyite and NATO alike but no more sustainable by evidence than the official Soviet version.

When Gorbachev opened the archives during *Glasnost*, in the mid 1980s, both 'totalitarians' and 'revisionists' claimed support from the new sources. Within the USSR, reappraisal of the Soviet leadership moved fast. Volkogonov's 'Russian Revisionist' biography *Stalin* (1991) contains much new detail but is similar to many Western ones in blaming Stalin for what went wrong.

The trickle from the archives became a flood when the USSR collapsed. These and the explosion of social, particularly local, history in Russia are likely to erode the Totalitarian model. However, the Totalitarian model of the USSR is useful to the elites of non-Russian republics and Russian Anti-Communists, so the debate is likely to continue.

FURTHER READING

This text has focused on the period 1925–41 because this seemed to be the critical period in shaping the nature of the Soviet regime. During the War, the system ossified and the postwar years repeat or continue earlier themes, rather than producing innovation.

The following are the titles referred to in this book:

Josef Stalin *The problems of Leninism* (Moscow, 1945)
Alexander Orlov *Secret history of Stalin's crimes* (Jarrold, 1954)
Walter Kritvisky *I was Stalin's agent* (Ian Faulkner, 1992)
Victor Kravchenko *I chose freedom* (Robert Hale, 1947)
Menshevik Nicolaevski 'Letters of an Old Bolshevik' in *Power and the Soviet elite* (Ann Arbor, 1965)
Leonard Shapiro *The Communist Party of the Soviet Union* (Eyre and Spottiswoode, 1960)
Fitzroy Maclean *Eastern Approaches* (Penguin, 1991)
Merle Fainsod *How Russia is ruled* (Cambridge University Press, 1965)
Trotsky *Revolution Betrayed* (Pathfinder, 1973)
Isaac Deutscher *Stalin: a political biography* (Penguin, 1966)
Robert Conquest *The Great Terror, a reassessment* (Hutchinson, 1986)
Nikita Khrushchev *Khrushchev Remembers* (Andre Deutsch, 1971)
Alexander Solzhenitsin *The Gulag Archipelago* (Collins Harvill, 1974)
Dimitri Volkogonov *Stalin* (Weidenfeld and Nicolson, 1991)

For the first-time reader the following texts are useful:

Michael Lynch *Stalin and Khrushchev* (Hodder and Stoughton, 1990) and Martin McCauley *Stalin and Stalinism* (Addison Wesley Longman, 1983) both cover the postwar years adequately. The latter includes some useful source material, as do Niall Rothnie's *Stalin and Russia* (Macmillan, 1991) and J Laver's *Russia 1914–1941* (Hodder and Stoughton, 1991).

For the reader who wants to go into more detail:

Chris Ward *Stalin's Russia* (Edward Arnold, 1993) is comprehensive, while Martin McCauley *The Soviet Union 1917–1991* (Addison Wesley Longman, 1993) and Edward Acton *Russia* (Addison Welsey Longman, 1986) provide good overviews. Sheila Fitzpatrick *The Russian Revolution* (Oxford University Press, 1982) is excellent up to 1932. Graeme Gill *Stalinism* (Macmillan, 1990) provides an accessible overview.

There is a wealth of specialist texts available.

Biographies
Robert Tucker *Stalin in Power* (Norton, 1992)
Alan Bullock *Hitler and Stalin: parallel lives* (HarperCollins, 1991)
Stephen Cohen *Bukharin* (Oxford University Press, 1980)

Collectivisation and Industrialisation
Moshe Lewin *The making of the Soviet System* (Methuen, 1985)
Alec Nove *An economic History of the USSR* (Penguin, 1992)
Davies, Harrison and Wheatcroft *The economic transformation of the Soviet Union* (Cambridge University Press, 1994)

Party and Purges
John Arch-Getty *Origins of the Great Purge* (Cambridge University Press, 1985)
Robert Conquest *The Great Terror, a reassessment* (Hutchinson, 1986)
Gábor Rittersporn *Stalinist simplifications* (Harwood, 1991)
John Arch-Getty and Roberta Manning *Stalinist Terror* (Cambridge University Press, 1993). This includes valuable case studies by Viola, Kuromiya and Starkov.

Foreign policy and World War Two
John Barber and Mark Harrison *The Soviet Home Front* (Addison Wesley Longman, 1991)
Geoffrey Roberts *The Soviet Union and the origins of the Second World War* (Macmillan, 1995)

Social history
Vladimir Andrle *A Social History of Twentieth-Century Russia* (Edward Arnold, 1994)

Other sources
The 1993 ITV documentary series 'Stalin' is particularly useful. Among the literature from and about the period, Mikhail Sholokov's *Virgin soil upturned* and Anatoli Rybakov's *Children of the Arbat* provide insights into collectivisation and the atmosphere of the Purges respectively. Peter Hopkirk's *Setting the East ablaze* (Oxford University Press, 1984) adds a valuable Asian dimension to the USSR in the 1920s.

INDEX

KEY TERMS

PROFILES

MAIN INDEX